COMMODITY SUPPLY MANAGEMENT BY PRODUCING COUNTRIES

UNU WORLD INSTITUTE FOR DEVELOPMENT ECONOMICS RESEARCH (UNU/WIDER) was established by the United Nations University as its first research and training centre and started work in Helsinki, Finland in 1985. The purpose of the institute is to undertake applied research and policy analysis on structural changes affecting the developing and transitional economies, to provide a forum for the advocacy of policies leading to robust, equitable and environmentally sustainable growth, and to promote capacity strengthening and training in the field of economic and social policy-making. Its work is carried out by staff researchers and visiting scholars in Helsinki and through networks of collaborating scholars and institutions around the world.

COMMODITY SUPPLY MANAGEMENT BY PRODUCING COUNTRIES

A Case-Study of the Tropical Beverage Crops

ALFRED MAIZELS
ROBERT BACON
GEORGE MAVROTAS

A study prepared for the World Institute for Development Economics Research of the United Nations University (UNU/WIDER)

CLARENDON PRESS · OXFORD
1997

Oxford University Press, Great Clarendon Street, Oxford OX2 6DP

Oxford New York
Athens Auckland Bangkok Bogota Bombay
Buenos Aires Calcutta Cape Town Dar es Salaam
Delhi Florence Hong Kong Istanbul Karachi
Kuala Lumpur Madras Madrid Melbourne
Mexico City Nairobi Paris Singapore
Taipei Tokyo Toronto
and associated companies in
Berlin Ibadan

Oxford is a trade mark of Oxford University Press

Published in the United States by
Oxford University Press Inc., New York

British Library Cataloguing in Publication Data
Data available

Library of Congress Cataloging-in-Publication Data
Maizels, Alfred.
Commodity supply management by producing countries : a case study
of the tropical beverage crops / by Alfred Maizels, Robert Bacon, George Mavrotas.
p. cm.—(UNU/WIDER studies in development economics)
"A study prepared for the World Institute for Developmental Economics
Research of the United Nations University (UNU/WIDER)."
Includes bibliographical references and index.
1. Coffee trade. 2. Tea trade. 3. Cocoa trade. 4. Tropical crops. 5. Tropics–Economic conditions.
I. Bacon, Robert William. II. Mavrotas, George. III. Title. IV. Series: Studies in development
economics.
HD9195.A2M34 1997 338. 1'737–dc21 96–52502

ISBN 0–19–823338–8

1   3   5   7   9   10   8   6   4   2

Typeset by Pure Tech India Ltd, Pondicherry
Printed in Great Britain by
Bookcraft (Bath) Ltd., Midsomer Norton, Avon

Contents

Contents   vii

STATISTICAL APPENDIX

List of Figures

List of Tables

List of Abbreviations

ACP	African, Caribbean and Pacific countries associated with the European Community (now Union)
ATPC	Association of Tin Producing Countries
CES	constant elasticity of substitution
FAO	Food and Agriculture Organization
GATT	General Agreement on Tariffs and Trade
GDP	gross domestic product
GNP	gross national product
ICA	International commodity agreement
ICCO	International Cocoa Agreement
ICO	International Coffee Agreement
IMF	International Monetary Fund
IPC	Integrated Programme for Commodities
ITC	International Tea Committee
OPEC	Organization of Petroleum Exporting Countries
SSA	Sub-Saharan Africa
UN	United Nations
UNCTAD	UN Conference on Trade and Development

Note: the $ symbol is used to indicate US dollars throughout.

Introduction

The idea for this book arose from the analysis of post-war trends in international commodity markets in an earlier study (Maizels, 1992). That analysis showed that whereas in the decades up to 1980 the main feature of these markets had been high short-term price instability, since that date the main feature has been a marked downward trend in real commodity prices (even though a number of important commodities continue to exhibit excessive short-term instability).

This change in the main characteristic of world commodity markets has had dramatically adverse effects on the export earnings of a large number of developing countries, on the size of their foreign debt, and on their ability to achieve significant progress in their development efforts. The policy implication, argued at some length in the earlier study, was that negotiations between developing and developed countries should be given high priority with the aim of evolving a viable and coherent set of measures to raise persistently depressed levels of commodity prices and commodity export earnings of developing countries. Such measures could be a key element in a renewed international strategy to accelerate the development process, particularly in low-income commodity-dependent countries.

International co-operation to deal with the commodity problems of developing countries has, however, been seriously eroded since the early 1980s. Over this period, the major developed countries have become increasingly opposed to any intervention in the international commodity markets, even to reduce high short-term price instability, which in earlier decades had been an agreed objective of both developed and developing countries. This important policy shift was a result of the advent of governments in the main developed countries intent on promoting the virtues of market forces for the solution of economic problems. As a consequence, these countries generally withdrew their support from the negotiation of commodity agreements for reducing high price instability, while they were also strongly opposed to market intervention to raise commodity prices above market trends, even though these trends were persistently downward. This opposition was strengthened by the fact that the developed countries benefited substantially from the relatively depressed prices of their commodity imports from developing countries.

With a continuing stalemate so far in the 1990s in international commodity policy, and continuing large foreign exchange losses by commodity-exporting developing countries as a result of a downward trend in real commodity prices, the question arises as to whether effective measures to regulate commodity supply could be taken by developing countries themselves to raise depressed prices to more remunerative levels for producing countries, while also achieving a medium-term balance between world supply and demand. The present study is an attempt to answer this question for one specific group of commodities—the tropical beverages— important for the export earnings of many developing countries. It analyses the problems that would arise, and the relative merits and drawbacks of alternative mechanisms that could be employed, to achieve the policy objective outlined above.

The analysis is based on detailed econometric models for each of the tropical beverages—cocoa, coffee, and tea—on the basis of which simulations are made of the effects of alternative schemes of supply management by the producing countries on market prices, production, consumption, stocks and export earnings. The simulations relate generally to the second half of the 1980s, though the results have clear implications for international commodity policy in the 1990s and beyond.

Plan of the book. Part I presents a review of the main commodity problems facing developing countries, and of the argument in favour of evolving appropriate supply management schemes.

The six chapters of Part I present the main findings of the study without the technical econometric analysis, which is given in Part II. The first chapter provides a general review of recent trends in exports of primary commodities from developing countries, focusing on the magnitude and impact of the downward trend in 'real' commodity prices on the foreign exchange earnings of each major developing region. This chapter also explains the rationale for selecting the tropical beverage crops for a case-study of the potential of supply management by producing countries as a mechanism for raising persistently depressed levels of commodity prices and commodity export earnings.

Chapter 2 reviews recent trends in the world markets for each tropical beverage, with an assessment of the various factors affecting market prices, as regards both short-term instability and longer-term trends. Chapter 3 contains a discussion of past international measures taken, and other proposed measures that have been considered, to improve the functioning of the world markets for each of the beverage crops. These measures have been directed essentially, but not solely, at reducing the degree of short-term price fluctuations. This chapter also contains a discussion of the new production regulation agreement within the framework of the International Cocoa Agreement, 1993, as well as of the new export retention scheme for coffee which has been in operation since October 1993 by the coffee-producing countries.

Given the need for some form of supply management, whether in the framework of an international agreement covering both producers and consumers, or operated by producing countries alone, Chapter 4 considers the relative merits and demerits of alternative schemes of supply management. The assumptions made for each assumed supply management scheme are set out in detail in Chapter 5, which also gives the quantitative results of the various model simulations, distinguishing—to the extent possible—the likely impact on each major producing country as well as on the world market as a whole. A summary of the main findings of the study, and of their implications for international commodity policy, is provided in Chapter 6.

Part II presents the econometric models for each of the tropical beverages, each being constructed from separate explanatory equations for the demand and supply sides of the world market, which are then used to form an integrated analysis of market price determination. The estimated equations of each model, as well as the simulation results, are included in the Appendix tables.

Acknowledgements. We are much indebted to Queen Elizabeth House, Oxford University, for providing a welcoming and supportive environment for this study, and to the World Institute for Development Economics Research (WIDER) of the United Nations University for funding. Special thanks are due to Professor Gerry Helleiner of Toronto University for many points of constructive criticism on the first draft of Part I and to an anonymous referee for a large number of other comments, criticisms, and suggestions, also on that draft. We have also benefited from the stimulating comments and suggestions of Dr Peter Greenhalgh of LMC International, Oxford, and Professor John Spraos of University College, London. The authors have also been helped substantially by suggestions and advice on data collection at the early stages of the study by Mr C. P. R. Dubois of the International Coffee Council, London. Secretarial assistance was supplied willingly and expeditiously by Karen Allsop, Anne Roche, and Bridget Smith.

I

World Market Trends and Supply Management Options

1

The International Economic Background

1.1 RECENT TRENDS IN INTERNATIONAL COMMODITY TRADE

Since the early 1980s a major feature of the world economy has been the emergence of wide disparities in the growth rates of different developing countries, disparities which had been very much smaller in earlier decades. At one extreme are the newly industrializing countries (NICs) of East Asia—South Korea, Taiwan, Hong Kong, and Singapore—which, together with China, achieved an average GDP growth rate of 9.0 per cent over the period from 1980 to 1991, and which now constitute a major new growth 'pole' in the world economy. At the other extreme, the developing countries of Sub-Saharan Africa averaged only 2.1 per cent a year growth, with per capita real product declining by over 10 per cent over the same period. While other developing regions fell into intermediate positions between these extremes, considerable disparities in growth rates emerged as between individual countries in these regions.

There are, of course, a large number of factors which influence the growth rates of individual developing countries including, in particular, their own economic and trade policies, the corresponding policies of their main trading partners as well as the latter's own growth rates, and the foreign exchange which they have available to purchase essential imports. It is this last element, foreign exchange availability, which has become of critical importance to a wide range of developing countries as a result of a sharp collapse in the prices of their primary commodity[1] exports in the early 1980s

---

[1] The terms 'commodity' or 'primary commodity' as used in this book exclude petroleum, which is a special case as regards market structure and price trends.

and the persistence of depressed commodity prices since then. Indeed, the heavy dependence of Sub-Saharan Africa on commodity exports contrasts sharply with the export pattern of the East Asian NICs which have become almost totally reliant on manufactured goods, prices of which have trended upward while their export volume has rapidly expanded. This difference in export patterns has undoubtedly been a major factor in the contrasting trends in the real export earnings of these two regions, and thereby also in their very different GDP growth rates.

The present book is focused on the developing countries which are important exporters of one group of primary commodities, namely the tropical beverage crops, cocoa, coffee, and tea. Before turning to examine the markets for these crops, however, it is useful to place them in a more general setting. Taking all non-oil commodities together, their dominant market feature since 1980 has been a persistent downward trend in real prices.[2] Between 1980 and 1992, real commodity prices (or the 'commodity terms of trade') fell by some 50 per cent to a new post-war low level—almost certainly lower, also, than the price nadir reached during the Great Depression of the 1930s.[3] The corresponding fall for real export unit values since 1980, at about 40 per cent, though less than the fall in market prices,[4] was none the less an adverse development of major magnitude for commodity-exporting countries.

The deterioration in the commodity terms of trade has been accompanied by a substantial increase in the volume of commodity exports from developing countries—a rise of about 50 per cent from 1980 to 1992, the greater part of this expansion having occurred since 1985 (Table 1.1). The GDP growth rate

[2] Real commodity prices are defined here as nominal market prices deflated by the UN index of unit value of manufactures exported by developed market-economy countries.

[3] Real commodity prices in 1992 were some 20% below the corresponding level in 1932, the low point of the inter-war depression, comparing the World Bank commodity price index for recent years with the annual price indices prepared by Grilli and Yang (1988) for the period from 1900 to 1986.

[4] For estimating terms of trade effects on export earnings, unit values (which cover all commodity exports) are more appropriate than any of the published price indices (which cover only a sample of exports with market quotations).

Table 1.1 *Terms of trade effects on commodity exports from developing countries, 1980–1992 (value of exports and terms of trade effects in $ bn.; indices based on 1980 = 100)*

	1980	1981–5	1986–8	1989–91	1992
Commodities					
Value of exports	109.0	98.5	112.8	135.5	136.3
Export indices:					
Value	100	90	103	124	125
Unit value	100	85	85	86	83
Volume	100	106	121	144	151
Manufactures					
Unit value	100	90	114	131	139
Commodity terms of trade	100	94	75	66	60
Terms of trade effects on commodity export earnings:					
Annual average	—	−5.3	−34.0	−54.2	−66.5
Cumulative from 1980	—	−27	−129	−292	−358

Notes: Figures are annual or annual averages.

manufactures unit value index relates to exports from developed market-economy countries (UN index).

commodity terms of trade index is unit value of commodity exports deflated by manufactures unit value index.

terms of trade effect is defined as $\sum_{i=1}^{n} V_{xi}\{1/Pm - 1/Px\}$, where $\sum_{i=1}^{n} V_{xi}$ denotes the value of commodity exports in any year subsequent to 1980, while P_m and P_x are respectively, the unit value of manufactures index and the unit value of commodities exports in that year, with base year (1980) unit value = 1.

Sources: UNCTAD *Commodity Yearbook*, 1989 and 1994; UN *Monthly Bulletin of Statistics* (various issues).

of the OECD countries—the major importers of commodities exported by developing countries, at about 2.5 per cent a year—was virtually the same in the first half of the 1980s as in the period 1986 to 1992, and in so far as changes in GDP indicate very approximately changes in demand for commodities in the short—and medium—term, this would imply that the failure of commodity unit values to recover from the depressed levels of the early 1980s has been predominantly the result of the supply expansion.[5]

---

[5] Recent IMF studies using econometric models confirm the predominance of supply movements in the determination of commodity price changes, particularly in the second half of the 1980s (Borensztein and Reinhart, 1994).

This combination of a fairly prolonged period of supply expansion with continuous decline in the commodity terms of trade would appear to be a perverse result, since in normal market conditions falling prices would be expected to result, at least in the medium term, in a decline in output, and not an increase. This points to the influence of one or more new elements in the commodity markets which were not operative before the mid–1980s, and which resulted in expansion in the volume of commodity exports from a wide range of developing countries.

One such new element after the mid–1980s was rising productivity for many staple crops, as well as diversification into export crops, such as the tropical beverages, following the relatively high prices received by producers towards the end of the 1970s, and supported in a number of cases by World Bank loans. For some commodities, particularly cocoa and coffee, the supply expansion resulted in the accumulation of large unsold stocks which added to the downward pressure on prices.

Second, the extreme shortage of foreign exchange experienced by most commodity-exporting countries—itself to a substantial extent the result of the downtrend in real commodity prices—led a large number of these countries to adopt export promotion measures, usually also a condition for IMF and World Bank financial support. The stabilization and structural adjustment programmes of these institutions usually included currency depreciation and other measures to promote exports. Such policies, however, if used simultaneously by many countries exporting the same commodity, are likely to result in an expansion in global export volume which only adds to the forces already depressing commodity prices. Third, since 1990 an additional factor depressing the prices of several important traded commodities has arisen as a result of the sharp contraction in industrial production, including arms production, in the former Soviet Union, and the consequent export of large quantities of surplus metals—particularly aluminium—on to the world market.

Since the mid–1980s, too, dollar unit values of manufactures exported by developed countries have risen substantially. Whereas these unit values were falling from 1980 to

1985 (by almost 15 per cent), after 1985 they began to rise fairly sharply (by nearly 60 per cent from 1985 to 1990). By 1992, unit values of manufactures had risen to some 40 per cent above the 1980 level, whereas for commodities the corresponding index was 15 per cent below 1980. This rise in unit value of manufactures appears to have been due, at least in part, to the sharp depreciation of the US dollar after 1985, which resulted in higher dollar prices for manufactures exported by Western Europe and Japan, though a continuing inflationary pressure in these industrial countries was likely to have been a contributing factor also.

For the commodity-exporting developing countries, these changes in the trends of unit values involved very large foreign exchange losses. Over the twelve years from 1980 to 1992, the cumulative loss on commodity exports amounted to almost $360 bn. (Table 1.1), which would appear to have been a major factor in the rise in the foreign debt of these countries, many of which were forced to borrow additional funds abroad to offset at least some of the foreign exchange loss.[6] A disquieting feature of the effects of the commodity terms of trade movement has been the progressive increase over the period in the resulting foreign exchange losses for the commodity-exporting countries. While in the first half of the 1980s, the annual rate of loss averaged $5 bn., this rose to $34 bn. in 1986–8, to almost $55 bn. in 1989–91, and to over $65 bn. in 1992 (which was significantly larger than the $58 bn. of official aid by OECD countries to developing countries and multilateral agencies in that year).

While corresponding estimates of the terms of trade losses on commodity exports could not be made for 1993 and 1994 at the time of writing (summer 1995), it would seem from the recent movements in commodity prices that the 1993 loss was

[6] The $350 bn. loss attributable to the deterioration in the commodity terms of trade of developing countries from 1980 to 1992 represents a substantial proportion of the increment in the public and publicly guaranteed foreign debt (excluding the debt of the major petroleum-exporting countries) over the same period of some $430 bn. Though these two figures are not strictly comparable—the total debt, for instance, reflects many other elements, such as debt cancellation and rescheduling—the comparison does indicate that the terms of trade deterioration was almost certainly a major element in the rise in the foreign debt of the commodity-exporting developing countries.

probably in the region of $65–70 bn., but for 1994 the loss was likely to have been significantly less as a result of the sharp rise in commodity prices in that year.

Of the various developing regions, easily the worst hit by the fall in real commodity prices has been Sub-Saharan Africa (SSA). This was partly because SSA is more heavily dependent on earnings from commodity exports than are other developing regions, and partly because SSA's largest single group of commodity exports, tropical beverage crops, suffered a greater fall in prices than any other major commodity group. Between 1980 and 1989–91, the unit value of SSA commodity exports had declined by some 25 per cent, as against falls of 17 per cent for Latin America, and only 10 per cent for South and South-East Asia, the two other major commodity-exporting developing regions (Table 1.2). Over this period, also, the volume of commodity exports from SSA rose by only 20 per cent, a substantially lower expansion than for South and South-East Asia (almost 60 per cent) and for Latin America (over 40 per cent). As a result, SSA was the only developing region which failed to see an increase in the dollar value of its commodity exports over the decade from 1980.

The foreign exchange loss attributable to the deterioration in the commodity terms of trade was, relatively to GDP, much greater for SSA than for the other developing regions (see bottom of Table 1.2.). For the years 1989–91, the annual average loss for SSA (over $8 bn. a year), represented 20 per cent of total SSA exports (including petroleum and manufactured goods) in 1990, and as much as 5 per cent of the region's GDP in that year. This is a huge loss by any standard; one comparison of interest would be the real income transfer from the OECD countries to the OPEC group in 1973–4 and again in 1978–9, as a result of the oil price 'shocks', amounting in each case to $2–2\frac{1}{2}$ per cent of the OECD countries' total GDP (OECD, 1980) The terms of trade 'shock' for SSA has been double that and, moreover, has been experienced by the poorest region of the world, least able to make the necessary structural adjustments.

For Latin America and the Caribbean, the deterioration in the commodity terms of trade in the 1980s was also very

Table 1.2 *Terms of trade effects on commodity exports from developing countries by region, 1980 to 1989–1991 (values and terms of trade effects in $ bn.; indices based on 1980 = 100)*

	Sub-Saharan Africa	Latin America and Caribbean	South and South-East Asia	Other developing regions	Totals
Value of exports					
1980	16.3	46.3	34.3	12.1	109.0
1989–91	15.0	54.8	48.9	16.7	135.5
Change	−1.3	8.5	14.6	4.6	26.5
Indices for 1989–91					
Value	92	118	143	138	124
Unit value	76	83	90	95	86
Volume	120	142	159	144	144
Terms of trade effects,					
1980 to 1989–91	−8.2	−24.2	−17.0	−4.9	−54.2
As propn. of 1990 GDP	−4.9	−2.2	−1.4	−0.4	−1.5

Notes and *Sources*: as Table 1.1.

substantial, this region accounting for about one-half of the total foreign exchange loss for all developing countries from 1980 to 1989–91. Though much smaller in relation to GDP than the loss for SSA, it was nevertheless large enough, at over 2 per cent of the region's GDP in 1990, to have had a major adverse impact on the external payments position. The corresponding terms of trade loss for South and South-East Asia in 1989–91 was in the region of $1\frac{1}{2}$ per cent of GDP, significantly lower than for Latin America, reflecting essentially the greater decline during the 1980s in the unit value of commodity exports from the latter region (Table 1.2.).

Throughout the 1980s and into the early 1990s, a large number of commodity-dependent developing countries have suffered from severe foreign exchange shortage, a result essentially of the downtrend in the real prices of their commodity exports, of high debt service payments, and of the virtual cessation of foreign loans from 1982 to the early 1990s. Many of these countries entered a phase of 'import strangulation', where domestic activity was constrained, or even contracted, as a result of lack of complementary imports such as spare parts, replacement equipment, and intermediate products. For such countries, the foreign exchange squeeze has resulted in a reduction in the efficiency of resource-use as well as in the level of domestic investment, both key elements for renewed economic growth. Over this period, also, the persistence of depressed levels of commodity prices has adversely affected government revenues in many developing countries where taxes on the export sector bulk large in total revenue. The contraction in government budgets in such countries has led to deteriorating provision, in both quantity and quality, of resources for the health, education, and other social sectors.

These various considerations raise a question as to whether the international community should consider alleviating the persisting foreign exchange constraint on the development of commodity-exporting countries, particularly the poorer among them, by adopting measures to raise depressed levels of prices of those commodities in structural oversupply, such as the tropical beverage crops. There already exists an international debt strategy designed to reduce the debt burden of low-income and other heavily indebted countries, but in the absence of a supporting strategy to reverse previous terms of trade losses on commodity exports which, as indicated earlier, constituted a major element in the debt build-up, it seems doubtful whether the present debt strategy can meet its objectives.

1.2   THE CONTINUING IMPASSE IN INTERNATIONAL COMMODITY POLICY

The underlying difficulty for the international community in evolving a policy to deal effectively with the market problems of commodities in structural oversupply is that since about 1980 a major divergence of views has emerged, as between developed (mainly commodity-importing) countries and developing (mainly commodity-exporting) countries as to the objectives to be attained by an international commodity policy, or even whether any such policy is desirable at all.

The main developed countries have traditionally been strongly opposed to any proposal which would involve raising commodity prices—even from depressed levels—above market trends. Moreover, while in earlier post-war decades these countries generally participated in international commodity agreements designed essentially to reduce excessive short-term price fluctuations (as distinct from raising the price trend), after the early 1980s they became increasingly hostile to such agreements. By 1990, only one such agreement, that for natural rubber, remained in existence, all the others— for sugar, cocoa, coffee, and tin—having collapsed or become non-operative.

Though the new international cocoa agreement concluded in 1993—and discussed further in Chapter 3—provides for the regulation of production within a framework of producer–consumer co-operation, this appears to be a special case, the developed countries remaining generally opposed to measures to regulate supply in order to raise depressed levels of commodity prices. There are several reasons for this. First, continuing low prices for their commodity imports have become an important element in the anti-inflationary domestic policies of many developed countries, which provides them with an incentive to maintain the present commodity situation so far as possible. A second factor is that the governments of several of the larger developed countries had, by about 1980, become keen advocates of the virtues of the 'free play of market forces' so that they were generally not in favour of intervention in the international commodity markets since, it was often argued, this would inevitably lead to overproduction and resource misallocation. A third consideration, at least for some developed country governments, has been that steps to alleviate the foreign exchange squeeze might well reduce the leverage of the Bretton Woods institutions in the application of strict conditionality terms to their stabilization and structural adjustment programmes.

The argument that market intervention to raise prices from free market levels will result in a misallocation of resources by encouraging unnecessary increases in production, and hence in a reduction in real income, is a well-established proposition of neoclassical economic theory. However, that theory is based on a number of unrealistic assumptions, viz. the existence of perfect competition, perfect foresight, perfect factor mobility and price flexibility, full employment, and the absence of externalities and of increasing returns to scale. Once these assumptions are relaxed, the neoclassical argument no longer holds. To take one important case where the neoclassical assumptions do not hold, many commodity markets are far from being perfectly competitive. Where the market structure is oligopolistic, or where the market is heavily influenced by national or international policies, decisions on investment, output, and prices can diverge substantially from those that would be obtained in a perfectly competitive market. The agricultural sector of the economies of the developed countries over the post-war period has been a prime example of resource misallocation as a result of heavy subsidies given to high-cost domestic production, totalling over $300 bn. a year in the early 1990s. Following the GATT Uruguay Round agreement, these subsidies are to be cut by about 20 per cent over a six-year period from the relatively high levels of the years 1986–8, so that substantial agricultural subsidies will continue after the agreed cuts are effected. Moreover, it can be shown that if demand elasticities are low, the 'deadweight' loss resulting from price raising by means of supply regulation will be negligible relative to the net gain in welfare resulting from the redistribution of income from relatively rich consumers in developed countries to poor producers in developing countries (Spraos, 1983).

1.3   PRODUCER-ONLY SUPPLY MANAGEMENT

None the less, if developed country governments continue to oppose measures designed to raise persistently depressed levels of commodity prices, even by modest amounts, the question that arises is whether it would be technically feasible for producing countries to adopt such measures themselves. This would be a 'second-best' approach, and would be more difficult to apply, other than to a limited range of commodities, than an agreement involving both producers and consumers. This is mainly because for many commodities

developing countries supply only a part of the world market,
while a wide range of their exports of industrial raw materials
face competition from synthetics or other substitutes in their
main end-uses. In either case, price-substitution elasticities
are likely to be high. However, for certain commodities meeting rather strict criteria, producer-only schemes, which
involve some form of regulation of supply coming on the
world market ('supply management') would be technically
feasible. A producer-only scheme can best be regarded as
preparing the way for a later producer–consumer agreement
once a reasonable long-term balance in the market has been
achieved.

The essential conditions for a successful supply management scheme for a given commodity, to be operated by producer countries themselves, are:

- A high proportion of actual, and of potential, output
  should be under the control of countries members of
  the scheme (there being significant entry costs for
  non-members).
- Demand for the commodity must be price-inelastic (in
  particular, there should be no close substitutes).
- Member countries should retain a high degree of
  commitment to the scheme, to avoid it being undermined by excess production or exports.
- The price objective should be relatively modest, so
  that it could be accepted as fair and reasonable by
  consumers.
- Policing the scheme should be relatively uncompli-
  cated and effective.

The first two conditions, which relate essentially to market
structure, are quite restrictive. As regards the first condition, a
list of possible commodities which would qualify can be
established on the basis that (i) developing countries account
for a high share—say, over 80 per cent—of world exports,
and (ii) that their real prices have been on a downward trend
over the past decade. This list would include the tropical
beverages and bananas in the food group, various vegetable
oils—coconut, palm, and palm kernel,—some important agricultural raw materials—natural rubber, jute and sisal, and a

number of minerals and metals, namely bauxite, nickel ore, and tin metal. However, many of these commodities can be eliminated as viable candidates for supply management by the producing countries, either because they face severe competition from synthetic substitues produced in developed countries (e.g. the agricultural raw materials), or from other competing products (e.g. vegetable oils produced in developed countries), or they represent only the first stage in an industrial process, the later stages of which are concentrated mainly in developed countries (e.g. bauxite and nickel ore are inputs into the production of aluminium and nickel metal respectively).

Of the remaining commodities, easily the largest by value is the tropical beverages group, exports of which from developing countries reached a peak of $20 bn. in 1986 when coffee prices were unusually high, but fell to some $10 bn. in 1992 and 1993 with coffee prices at 60–5 per cent below the 1986 peak. Other possible candidates for producer supply management would be natural rubber and tin. For natural rubber an international price-stabilization agreement has been in operation since 1979, the latest renegotiation of which will cover the four years from 1996, using a buffer stock to keep prices within an agreed range. So long as producer–consumer co-operation continues to be effective in reducing rubber price instability, it would seem unlikely that producing countries would wish to establish their own scheme to raise the level of prices. For tin, a supply management scheme is already in place, operated by the main producing countries in order to reduce the large stock overhang in the world tin market which had accumulated before the collapse of the International Tin Agreement in 1985. This scheme has so far been only partially successful in raising prices from the low levels reached after the collapse of the Agreement, mainly as a result of increased exports from China (which joined the scheme only in 1994).

Thus, it would seem that—apart from rubber and tin—the tropical beverages are the most promising from the viewpoint of supply management by producers. There are several reasons for this. First, as already indicated, the producing countries can effectively regulate supply if they act jointly to do so. Second, the price-elasticity of world demand for these beverages is relatively very low, which allows a small reduction in supply to result in a more than proportionate increase in price and export earnings. Third, since tropical beverages account for a significantly higher proportion of export earnings of countries in Sub-Saharan Africa than in other developing regions, measures which raise prices from depressed levels would result in a relatively greater foreign exchange benefit to the poorest region. Fourth, the tropical beverages have suffered more than other commodity groups from the downtrend in prices since 1980, while being also a major contributor to the foreign exchange loss attributable to the deterioration in the terms of trade of commodity-dependent developing countries over this period. For all these reasons, the tropical beverages were selected as a case-study in the possible application of supply management by producer countries, which forms the subject of the present book.

The method of analysis, for each beverage, has been to develop a computable econometric model of the working of the world market, incorporating equations for production and consumption in each major trading country, together with equations linking the world price to the domestic producer price in the principal producing countries. These models aimed to cover the period from 1963 to 1990 (or 1991), though for many variables shorter periods had to be used owing to gaps in the available statistics. These models were then used to simulate the effects of alternative possible supply management schemes on the major economic variables, i.e. production, consumption, stocks, prices, and export earnings, the simulations covering the second half of the 1980s, which was the period of the sharpest fall in real prices.

The econometric analysis and simulations were carried out just before the conclusion of the International Cocoa Agreement, 1994, and before the entry into force in late 1993 of the export retention scheme for coffee operated by the producer countries, both of which are discussed in greater detail in Chapter 3. Though the specific mechanisms adopted in these two schemes are not exactly the same as any of the alternative schemes assumed in the simulations, they do indicate that the simulation results of the present study should prove useful as a quantitative guide to the probable outcomes of future supply management operations for these commodities.

2

Problems of the World Markets for Tropical Beverages

2.1 UNDERLYING ECONOMIC PROBLEMS

The world markets for the tropical beverage crops have a particular interest for international economic policy for two main reasons. First, because as already indicated, the majority of the producing countries are small, poor, and underdeveloped, so that changes in market conditions affecting the prices of tropical beverages, and the earnings of producing countries from their export, can thus have a major impact on incomes, employment, and living standards in a wide range of developing countries. Sub-Saharan Africa, which relies on exports of these beverage crops to a much greater extent than do other developing regions, is particularly vulnerable to adverse trends in tropical beverage prices.

Second, the markets for tropical beverages have traditionally been among the most unstable of the world markets for primary commodities, with sharp and unpredictable short-term price cycles, and consequent intermittent instability and uncertainty in the export revenues of producing countries. At the same time, world demand for these beverage crops is very price-inelastic, and it is this characteristic which makes them suitable for some form of international supply management designed to reduce their short-term market fluctuations and/or to raise depressed levels of prices.

An important distinction needs to be made at the outset between the raw forms of these beverage crops, such as cocoa or coffee beans, and the processed or manufactured forms. Several stages of processing may exist, as for cocoa, from cocoa beans to intermediate products (cocoa powder, cocoa paste, and cocoa butter), and to cocoa manufactures (primarily chocolate, but including also other food preparations

containing cocoa or chocolate). For coffee, the principal processed product is instant coffee, though the production of
coffee extracts, essences, and concentrates is also of some
significance. For tea, processed forms include iced tea preparations and instant tea, while the blending of different
varieties is, in effect, an important form of processing. For
all three beverages, exports from developing countries have
traditionally consisted almost entirely of the raw forms, with
processing and manufacturing stages being the preserve of
developed countries importing cocoa or coffee beans, or bulk
tea.

For both coffee and tea, developing country exports still
consist essentially of the raw forms. In 1990, for example,
processed coffee represented only 5 per cent of all coffee
exports from these countries, while the proportion was even
smaller for tea. However, noticeable progress has been made
in this regard in the case of cocoa exports, for which processed and manufactured forms increased from 20 per cent in
1975 to 27 per cent during 1980–2, and to 31 per cent in 1990–
2. Almost all of this trade, however, is in intermediate products, chocolate and other foods containing cocoa accounting
for only 4 per cent by value in 1990–2.[1]

A shift into processed forms would bring benefit to producing countries, in so far as it would represent value added
which increases their national income and foreign exchange
earnings, after allowing for the cost of imported inputs, and
of associated royalties and other payments, if any, for licensed
technology. However, the development of viable processing
and manufacturing stages for the tropical beverage industries
in developing countries on any substantial scale would
appear to be one of gradual evolution over the long term.
The present book is concerned essentially with the immediate
and short-term difficulties of developing countries arising
from their dependence on foreign exchange earned by the
export of the tropical beverage crops. Since, as already
noted, these exports are largely (cocoa) or mainly (coffee
and tea) in the unprocessed forms of these crops, the study
is necessarily confined to these.

[1] UNCTAD (1994), table A.6. The percentages as published relate to
imports of cocoa and coffee into developed market-economy countries.

The major problems faced by countries exporting the raw forms of the tropical beverage crops arise from (i) the unusually high short-term fluctuations in their prices on world markets, and (ii) the persistence since the beginning of the 1980s of depressed levels of prices. The degree of short-term price *instability* of each beverage crop is shown in Table 2.1, in relation to the price instability of non-oil primary commodities as a whole. Over both the 1960s and 1970s the instability index for tropical beverages was some two-thirds higher than the average for all commodities. The instability indices for both cocoa and coffee during these two decades far exceeded those for the great majority of other traded commodities, only five[2] of which had instability indices which exceeded those for cocoa and coffee. Since the early 1980s, however, commodity price instability has moderated somewhat, though still remaining high for a number of important commodities, including coffee and, to a lesser extent, cocoa and tea.

Table 2.1 *Price instability and price trends for tropical beverages and for all commodities, 1962–1991 (per cent variation for instability index; per cent p.a for price trend)*

	Tropical beverages				All commodities
	Cocoa	Coffee	Tea	Total	
Instability index:					
1962–80	27.7	28.4	20.9	25.5	15.2
1980–6	11.1	11.8	19.3	10.4	8.2
1986–91	9.1	16.8	9.9	10.0	8.5
Trend in real price:					
1962–80	5.7	2.9	−3.3	2.9	1.1
1980–6	−0.3	3.6	0.5	1.7	−7.3
1986–91	−19.1	−21.1	−1.8	−17.8	−0.5

Notes: Instability index is mean annual percentage deviation from exponential trend; real price is current price deflated by UN index of export unit value of manufactures exported by developed market-economy countries. Figures for 'all commodities' exclude petroleum.

Sources: as Table 1.1.

[2] These were sugar, linseed oil, sisal, tungsten, and phosphate rock, out of the 43 commodities included in UNCTAD's monthly commodity price index (see UNCTAD 1992, table A.2.).

By contrast, the *trend* of real prices of tropical beverages, which had been moderately upward in the 1960s and 1970s—and even in the first half of the 1980s the trend was still marginally upward—by the second half of the decade a very sharp deterioration had come to dominate the market situation and outlook for these beverage crops (Table 2.1).

For all three beverages, the declines in nominal prices after 1985 reflected a faster growth in supply than in consumption, with the accumulation of large unsold stocks in the case of cocoa and coffee. Prices had been relatively high towards the end of the 1970s, encouraging new plantings, much of which consisted of high-yield varieties. In addition, diversification programmes in certain countries—especially in Malaysia (cocoa), Kenya (tea), and Indonesia (coffee and tea)—were important elements in the expansion in world supply, while the acceptance by a large number of producing countries of IMF stabilization programmes has involved, *inter alia*, the raising of prices in domestic currencies received by producers which, in turn, encouraged the expansion of production and exports, thus adding to the depressive forces at work in the world market.

In addition, after 1985 there was a substantial rise in the unit value of manufactures exported by developed countries, to a large extent the result of the depreciation of the US dollar. This, combined with the fall in nominal dollar prices of the tropical beverages, caused a sharp decline in real prices of both cocoa and coffee, by about 20 per cent a year, on average, over the years 1986 to 1991. This was a contrast to the experience of most other primary commodities, for which real prices declined appreciably over the first half of the 1980s, but showed relatively little change, on balance, over the second half of that decade (Table 2.1).

Though a number of similar factors have been at work in the three tropical beverage markets contributing to substantial short-term price instability, or to the downward trend in real prices over the past decade, there have also been a number of differences in the influences of climatic and other factors which necessitate a closer examination of each market separately.

2.2   THE COCOA MARKET

Cocoa cultivation is restricted to a limited range of countries because of its particular growth conditions. In 1992, for example, eight developing countries accounted for over 85 per cent of world cocoa bean production, and over 80 per cent of world cocoa bean exports. On the demand side, the cocoa market is concentrated in the developed countries, with the USA and the European Community together accounting for almost 80 per cent of world cocoa bean imports in 1992. This double concentration imparts a substantial degree of uncertainty and instability into the cocoa market, which is thereby made vulnerable to sudden or unforeseen changes in output due to climatic variations or other causes in one or other producing country, and to business cycle movements and the changing use of cocoa substitutes in a relatively small number of consuming countries.

The volatility inherent in the world market for cocoa arising from its concentrated geographical structure is reinforced by two other market features. The first is the low price-elasticities of both demand and supply, especially in the short term, which result in a considerably larger proportionate change in price than in output or exports. Moreover a time-lag in the response of supply to an increase in market prices (as a result of the gestation period involved in new plantings) is likely to create an oversupply situation in future periods if demand has failed to expand proportionately in the interim. Conversely, the lag in supply response to a fall in prices will create a shortage later if demand by then has increased. Thus, supply lags tend to result in price cycles and consequent uncertainty, particularly where demand is itself subject to short-term variability.

The second element adding to short-term fluctuations in the cocoa market is the flow of speculative funds into and out of cocoa futures contracts traded on the terminal markets (which are mainly in London and New York). To the extent that speculators follow a 'herd instinct' and buy (sell) when prices are rising (falling), they will amplify the price fluctuations arising from fluctuations on the supply and demand sides of the 'real' market for physical cocoa.

The factors behind the movement in world cocoa prices in recent decades are examined in some detail in Chapter 7, where the relative importance of supply and demand influences are assessed on the basis of an econometric model. It suffices here to mention that the sharp decline in cocoa prices since the mid-1980s was essentially due to the faster growth of world production than of world consumption, which led to a rapid accumulation of stocks. Over the second half of the 1980s substantial surpluses appeared, leading to a sharp rise in stocks from an average of some 600 thousand tonnes during 1983–6 to double that level by 1987–9. The corresponding rise in the stocks/grindings ratio was from 33 to 57 per cent (Table 2.2). The peak stock level, at over 1.5m. tonnes, was reached at the end of the 1990–1 crop-year, followed by declines thereafter to an estimated 1.2m. tonnes at the end of the 1994–5 season as world consumption began to overtake production.

The close association between changes in the stock/grindings ratio and cocoa prices can be seen in Figure 2.1. The rise in this ratio from 1984 to 1991, from 28 to 67 per cent, was

Table 2.2 *World cocoa balance sheet, 1979–1994 (1000 tonnes; percentages for stocks/grindings ratio)*

	1979–82	1983–6	1987–9	1990–2	1993–4
Production	1,657	1,862	2,357	2,389	2,434
Grindings	1,567	1,830	2,106	2,355	2,522
Surplus/deficit	73	14	227	10	−113
Total end-of-season stocks	679	606	1,194	1,504	1,308
Stocks/Grindings ratio	43	33	57	64	52

Notes: Years are crop years beginning 1 Oct. of year shown; 1979 e.g., stands for crop year 1979–80. Figures are annual averages for periods shown.

Surplus/deficit is production (less 1% for loss in weight) minus grindings.

Figures for 1994 (crop year 1994–5) are forecasts made in mid–1995 by the International Cocoa Organization.

Total stocks include ICCO buffer stock.

Source: *Quarterly Bulletin of Cocoa Statistics* (various issues), International Cocoa Organization, London.

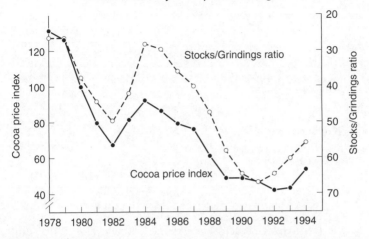

Fig. 2.1 Relationship between cocoa stocks/grinding ratio (per cent, with scale inverted) and cocoa price indices, 1980=100), 1978–94

Notes: The stocks/grindings ratio relates total end-of-season stocks (at 30 Sept.) to grindings in year commencing previous 1 Oct. The cocoa price relates to calendar year averages.

Sources: *Quarterly Bulletin of Cocoa Statistics* (various issues), International Cocoa Organization, London; UNCTAD *Monthly Commodity Price Bulletin* (various issues), Geneva.

associated with a fall of some 50 per cent in the cocoa price, while the subsequent decline in the ratio from 1991 to 1994 was accompanied by a modest recovery in cocoa prices, reflecting a continuation of the previous relationship between these two variables.

The fall in world cocoa prices, which was only partially offset by the expansion in the volume of cocoa exports from producing countries which rose by 60 per cent over the decade of the 1980s, has had serious adverse effects on their cocoa export earnings. Some part of the loss in the first half of the 1980s resulting from the fall in cocoa prices was offset by declines in prices of manufactures imported from developed countries, but after 1985 the dollar prices of these imports rose as cocoa prices continued to fall. None the less, it was the sharp decline in cocoa prices which accounted for the major part of the terms of trade loss since 1985 (see Table 2.3).

Table 2.3 *Change in value of cocoa exports from developing countries in
relation to terms of trade effect, 1980–1993 (values in $ bn.)*

	1980	1981–5	1986–8	1989–91	1992–3
Value of cocoa exports	3.76	3.07	3.80	2.88	2.44
Change from 1980	—	−0.69	0.04	−0.88	−1.32
of which:					
Unit value change	—	−1.29	−1.37	−3.31	−3.79
Volume change	—	0.60	1.41	2.43	2.47
Terms of trade effect	—	−0.92	−1.90	−3.99	−4.45
As % of 1980 export					
value	—	−24	−51	−106	−118

Notes: Cocoa exports include beans plus cocoa products.

Figures are annual or annual averages.

Unit value change is actual export value minus value at 1980 unit
value. Volume change is movement in export value at 1980 unit
value.

Terms of trade effect is defined in Notes to Table 1.1.

Sources: as Table 1.1.

The fall in real cocoa prices after 1985 caused a market
deterioration in the real foreign exchange earnings of cocoa-
exporting countries. While the terms of trade effect over the
period 1981–5 had been an annual average loss of $0.9bn.
(one-quarter of the 1980 export value), the corresponding
loss in 1986–8 had risen to $1.9bn. (one-half of the 1980
total), and rose further to $4.0bn. in 1989–1 (exceeding the
1980 figure), and to almost $4.5bn. in 1992 (nearly 20 per cent
higher than in 1980). The annual movement in the rate of loss
attributable to the terms of trade deterioration for cocoa
exports can be seen in Figure 2.2 (which covers all three
tropical beverage crops).

These foreign exchange losses resulting from the fall in
cocoa prices have been particularly serious for those countries
heavily dependent on cocoa for a substantial part of their
export earnings. In 1988—the year in which the International
Cocoa Agreement collapsed—cocoa, including processed
forms, accounted for 46 per cent of export earnings for
Ghana, 30 per cent for Côte d'Ivoire, and 24 per cent for
Cameroon. By 1993, the fall in cocoa prices from the 1988
level had resulted in a loss of foreign exchange in 1993 of

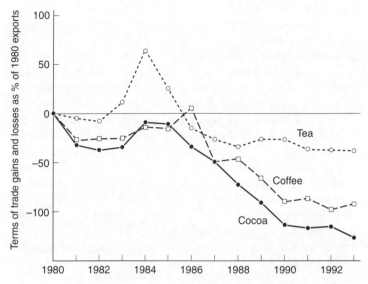

Fig. 2.2 Terms of trade gains and losses on exports of tropical beverages, 1980–93
Sources: As for Table 1.1.

almost $300m. for Ghana (representing about 30 per cent of total merchandise exports in 1988), over $650m. for Côte d'Ivoire (about 25 per cent), and $60m. for Cameroon (7 per cent). For these countries, the movement in world cocoa prices remains a major determinant of their ability to develop their economies. For other producing countries, dependence on cocoa is relatively small, though cocoa remains of some significance as an earner of foreign exchange, and as a contributor to domestic output and employment.

2.3   THE COFFEE MARKET

Coffee is a tropical crop which can be cultivated in a considerable number of countries, in Latin America—the main producing region—as well as in Africa, Asia, and Oceania. However, the supply of coffee is heavily dominated by Brazil, traditionally by far the largest producing country, and

Colombia; together they have accounted for about 40 per cent of world coffee exports in recent years. Arabica and robusta are the two most important species of coffee, arabica being grown throughout Latin America, in Central and East Africa, in India, and to some extent in Indonesia, while robusta is grown in West and Central Africa, throughout South-East Asia, and to some extent in Brazil.

On the demand side, the main consuming markets are the developed countries. The European Community and the USA together account for over 50 per cent of total world coffee consumption, with a further 15 per cent in other developed market-economy countries. Coffee consumption in the developing countries has been growing less fast than the world total in recent years; in 1985, the developing countries accounted for 29 per cent of world coffee consumption, the corresponding proportion for 1990 being 27 per cent. Brazil is easily the largest coffee consumer among producing countries, accounting for 9–10 per cent of the world total.

While the wide geographic spread of coffee production tends to result in intense competition among producers, particularly within each main species of coffee, large transnational corporations have built up considerable market power on the demand side. Transnational corporations have also come to dominate sales of roast and soluble coffee, marketed under apparently competing trade names in virtually all the developed countries. It has been estimated that four transnationals accounted in 1978 for one-third of the world market for roast and ground coffee,[3] and as much as four-fifths of the market for soluble coffee (which represents about 20 per cent of all coffee sold). Market dominance in sales of processed coffee (roast, ground, and soluble) also acts as an effective barrier to the development or expansion of production and exports of processed forms by developing coffee-producing countries, which generally remain heavily dependent on the vagaries of the world market for unprocessed coffee.[4]

[3] See UNCTAD (1984).
[4] Brazil, the largest coffee-producing country is, however, an exception, since its coffee exports in all forms account for only about 5% of total merchandise exports.

Short-term price fluctuations

The world market for unprocessed coffee has indeed been traditionally subject to substantial short-term price fluctuations. Several factors have contributed to this outcome. First, as with other tropical beverage crops, both demand and supply are characterized by low price-elasticities, especially in the short term, so that relative variation in price is substantially greater than in physical supply. Moreover, there is a gestation period of 3–4 years before new plantings begin to yield coffee berries, so that an oversupply situation can be created in future periods if demand has failed to expand proportionately in the interim. Conversely, as mentioned earlier, the lag in supply response to a fall in prices will create a shortage later if demand by then has increased.

Second, there is also a biennial cycle in yield from coffee trees and bushes, which may or may not coincide with the fluctuation in supply resulting from the gestation period of new plantings, thus adding to uncertainties in the market and to the amplitude of short-term price variation.

A third element is the susceptibility of coffee to damage by frost. Occasional seasonal frosts in some of the main coffee-growing areas of Brazil have resulted in fears that the coming harvest was likely to be short, a sentiment which induced sharp rises in coffee prices in the main trading centres in advance of the harvest for that year. Serious frost damage, as in 1975, can result in substantial shortfalls in world coffee production, which may take several years to rectify. Here, again, frost damage may or may not coincide with market movements, so that upward or downward price cycles may be accentuated or mitigated, depending on circumstances.

Fourth, as for cocoa, the flow of speculative funds into and out of coffee futures contracts on the London and New York terminal markets can substantially accentuate the short-term variations in price. To the extent that speculators follow a 'herd instinct' and buy (sell) when prices are rising (falling), they will amplify the price fluctuations arising from variations in supply and demand for physical coffee.

Price trend

As already mentioned, there was a marked deterioration in the trend of coffee prices after 1986, and the main factors involved are explored further in Chapter 8. As Table 2.4 indicates, the world coffee market was in modest surplus in the later 1970s. However, during the 1980s a large and persistent overproduction of coffee emerged as new plantings came into bearing. Stocks (held mostly in producer countries) which had represented some 60 per cent of consumption at the end of the 1970s, rose substantially to over 80 per cent a decade later. This rise in the level of unsold stocks was clearly an important factor in the downward trend in coffee prices over the past decade, as can be seen from Figure 2.3, which juxtaposes the movement in coffee prices with that in the stocks/consumption ratio (on an inverted scale) for the period 1978 to 1994. The quantitative relationship between these two variables is examined in detail in Chapter 8.

The impact on coffee export earnings

The fall in real coffee prices (or, to use an equivalent term, the deterioration in the coffee terms of trade) has had a catastrophic effect on the export earnings of those coffee-producing countries heavily dependent on this beverage crop.

Table 2.4   *World coffee balance sheet, 1976–1994*
(million bags of 60 kg.)

	1976–9	1980–4	1985–8	1989–91	1992–4
Production	73.9	89.3	92.5	95.4	88.2
Consumption	65.9	73.4	76.6	81.0	81.4
Surplus	8.0	15.9	15.9	14.4	6.8
End-of-season stocks	38.6	55.0	63.6	68.9	53.0
Stocks/consumption ratio	59	75	83	85	65

Notes: Figures are annual averages for years beginning 1 Oct. e.g. '1976' indicates year 1976–7. Production figures are world totals, consumption figures are totals for member countries of ICO.

Source: International Coffee Organization, London.

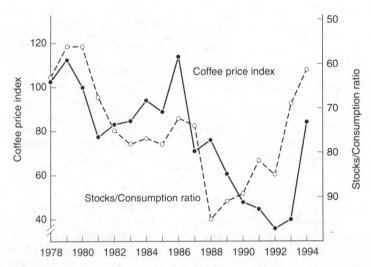

Fig. 2.3 Relationship between coffee stocks/consumption ratio (per cent., with scale inverted) and coffee price (indices, 1980=100), 1978–94

Notes: The stocks/consumption ratio relates total end-of-season stocks in ICO member countries (at 30 Sept.) to consumption in year beginning previous 1 Oct. The price index relates to the Composite Indicator Price of the 1979 International Coffee Agreement.

Source: UNCTAD *Monthly Commodity Price Bulletin* (various issues), Geneva; International Coffee Organization, London.

As for cocoa, the loss of export revenue resulting from the decline in nominal coffee prices over the first half of the 1980s was partly offset by the fall in the unit value of manufactures exported by developed countries. On a net basis, the foreign exchange loss due to the terms of trade deterioration amounted to $2.6bn. a year, on average, for the years 1981–4, and to $2.9bn. a year for 1985–8. However, in subsequent years the corresponding loss rose sharply, to $9.4bn. in 1989–91, and further to $10.9bn. in 1992–3 (Table 2.5). The rate of deterioration over the period since 1980 was much the same for coffee as for cocoa (see Figure. 2.1). For the whole period, 1981–93, the cumulative coffee terms of trade loss amounted to $72bn., representing some six times the value of all coffee exports from developing countries in 1980.

Table 2.5 *Change in value of coffee exports from developing countries in relation to terms of trade effect, 1980–1993 (values in $ bn.)*

	1980	1981–4	1985–8	1989–91	1992–3
Value of coffee exports	11.63	8.81	10.68	7.09	5.13
Change from 1980	—	−2.82	−0.95	−4.54	−6.50
of which:					
Unit value change	—	−3.58	−2.43	−7.71	−9.50
Volume change	—	0.76	1.48	3.17	3.00
Terms of trade effect	—	−2.61	−2.88	−9.36	−10.89
As % of 1980 exports	—	−22	−25	−80	−94

Notes and *Sources*: as Table 1.1.

There was an exceptionally large proportionate fall in coffee export earnings between 1989 and 1990, precipitated by the collapse of the export quota system of the International Coffee Agreement in the summer of 1989 (though, as already indicated, the underlying cause was the faster growth in world coffee production than in coffee consumption). Comparing coffee exports in 1990, the first post-quota year with 1988, the last quota year, there was a decline of $2.6bn., but allowing for the increase in export volume, the loss attributable to the coffee price collapse amounted to almost $4bn.

Over this period, individual country experiences varied widely. The three countries most heavily dependent on coffee are Uganda (coffee accounting for over 95 per cent of total exports in recent years), Burundi (over 85 per cent), and Rwanda (over 75 per cent). In all three countries, the loss of export earnings attributable to the fall in coffee prices accounted for virtually all, or more than, the decline in total export value (Table 2.6). Ethiopia was exceptional inasmuch as the magnitude of the negative price effect was considerably exceeded by a sharp fall in export volume—reflecting economic dislocation in that country's civil war—while for Tanzania the fall in coffee earnings was more than offset by an increase in other exports. Of the coffee-dependent Central American countries, three—El Salvador, Honduras, and Nicaragua—suffered significant reductions both in coffee, and total, export earnings. Colombia, with a fairly diversified economy, benefited from a rise in the price of its petroleum

Table 2.6 *Effect of coffee price fall on export earnings of coffee-dependent countries, 1988–1992 (coffee share in per cent; other figures in $ m.)*

	Coffee share of total exports	Coffee exports					Total exports
		1988	1992	Change, 1988–92			Change, 1988–92
	1988			Value	Unit value	Volume	
Africa							
Burundi	86	115	48	−67	−76	9	−58
Ethiopia	65	273	109	−164	−36	−128	−252
Madagascar	27	74	32	−42	−52	10	−7
Rwanda	76	77	35	−42	−49	7	−33
Tanzania	46	123	69	−54	−98	44	168
Uganda	97	265	95	−170	−124	−46	−131
Latin america							
Colombia	33	1,641	1,261	−380	−1,536	1,156	2,026
El Salvador	59	358	148	−210	−207	−3	−54
Guatemala	41	419	248	−171	−233	62	273
Honduras	24	200	108	−92	−113	21	−41
Nicaragua	36	85	46	−39	−55	16	−15

Notes: The unit value element of the change in value is defined as $V_{x1}\{1 - 1/P_{x1}\}$, where V_{x1} = value of coffee exports in 1992, and P_{x1} = unit value index of coffee exports in 1992, with the base year (1988) index = 1.

The table includes all countries for which the share of coffee in total exports in 1988 exceeded 20%.

Source: UNCTAD *Commodity Yearbook*, 1994.

exports, which greatly exceeded the fall in coffee export revenue.

The fall in world coffee prices has also been passed back, to a greater or lesser extent, to coffee farmers, who have been producing at a loss in many countries. According to a market analyst, most Latin American arabica producers needed a price of 100 US cents a lb. in 1991 in order to break even, whereas the average market price in that year was 90 cents for Colombian mild and 85 cents for other mild coffee. For African robusta producers, he estimated that they would need 60 cents a lb. to 'make a modest profit', whereas the average market price for robusta coffee in 1991 was only 50 cents.[5] One

[5] *Financial Times*, 20.9.1991.

result of the sharp decline in profitability of coffee production in recent years has been the uprooting of older and less productive coffee bushes, the reduced use of fertilizer, and the growing of alternative crops, or turning to cattle grazing, in order to diversify risks.[6] One effect has been a tendency to lower the average quality of coffee produced in many traditional coffee-growing areas, a consequence which is not in the long-term interests of either producers or consumers.

2.4   THE TEA MARKET

The world market for tea is highly concentrated, both by country of origin and of ultimate consumption. Tea cultivation is concentrated mainly in South Asia, China, and East Africa, these three areas together accounting for some 70 per cent of world tea production in 1991. Apart from Japan and the former Soviet Union (together producing a further 7 per cent), the remaining 20 per cent came almost entirely from developing countries in Asia (mainly Turkey and Iran) and Latin America (mainly Argentina).

There is a large variety of tea, depending on local climate, altitude of cultivation, condition of soil, and cultivation practices, and thus a considerable variation in quality as perceived by tea traders, blenders, and ultimate consumers. There are two major types, catering to very different markets, namely black tea and green tea. Black tea is the predominant type traded on the world market, accounting for over 90 per cent of total trade in tea. However, because of the inadequacy of the available statistics of production and trade in green tea, the present study relates to all tea. The inclusion of green tea is not likely to have resulted in significant bias in the analysis.

Several of the major tea-producing countries have large domestic tea consumption, particularly China and Japan, as well as the countries of the former Soviet Union, Iran,

[6] For example, the number of coffee trees in Brazil had been reduced from 4.2bn. in 1988 to 3.2bn. by mid-1992, while a survey by the National Coffee Council, published in May 1992, showed that 55% of coffee plantations were in a poor state, while a further 35% were judged unsatisfactory (ibid., 7 May 1992).

and Turkey. Domestic consumption in these countries is not directly related to changes in the supply–demand balance in the world tea market, so that a more accurate picture of the market can be had by focusing on their foreign trade in tea.

Two major features of the trends in world tea trade since the mid-1970s are evident (Table 2.7). First, total world demand, as indicated by world imports, has risen at a fairly uniform, though relatively low, growth rate of 2.3 per cent a year. Second, some major structural changes have taken place over the past two decades in the relative importance of both different import markets, and different sources of supply.

Table 2.7 *World trade in tea, 1976–1993 (total exports and imports in million tonnes; country trade as per cent of total)*

	1976–9	1980–4	1985–8	1989–91	1992–3
Exports					
Total developing					
countries	0.81	0.91	1.03	1.14	1.08
of which:					
China	9.2	12.3	16.6	17.0	17.6
Kenya	10.5	10.4	14.1	14.8	16.5
India	26.0	23.8	19.6	18.1	15.6
Indonesia	6.4	8.1	8.6	9.8	11.4
Sri Lanka	23.4	20.1	20.2	18.4	14.7
Imports					
World total	0.87	0.93	1.07	1.17	1.23
of which:					
Developed market					
economies	53.1	48.2	41.1	37.7	41.8
(UK)	(24.4)	(21.4)	(17.7)	(15.6)	(16.4)
Developing countries	37.9	40.0	43.8	42.1	45.7
(Asia)	(23.2)	(25.9)	(27.7)	(27.3)	(28.8)
Eastern Europe and	9.0	11.9	15.0	20.2	12.6
former Soviet Union					

Notes: The figures are annual averages. The totals for developing countries include China and Viet Nam. Tea exports from developed market-economy countries are not included, as these are almost entirely re-exports.

Sources: UNCTAD *Commodity Yearbooks*, 1984, 1987, and 1994.

On the supply side, the former dominance of India and Sri Lanka has been ended as the result of the rapid growth of tea exports from China, Kenya, and Indonesia, combined with relative stagnation in the volume of tea exports from India and Sri Lanka. Tea production in India, the largest producer, rose by some 300,000 tonnes (about 70 per cent) over the two decades up to 1990, but the whole of this expansion was taken up by domestic sales to meet the rapid growth in home demand.

On the demand side, the main changes over the past two decades have been the decline of the UK as the pre-eminent market, and the expansion of the market for imported tea in Asian countries. Tea consumption in the UK, traditionally the largest import market, has been on a downward trend since the late 1950s; per capita consumption peaked at 4.6 kg. in 1958, but by 1970 had fallen to 4.0 kg., to 3.2 kg. by 1980, and to 2.5 kg. by 1990. From 1980 to 1990, apparent consumption of tea in the UK fell by 44,000 tonnes (24 per cent), while for other developed market-economies as a group the corresponding decline was 16,000 tonnes (13 per cent), the entire fall being in Australia, Canada, and South Africa. By contrast, the developing countries as a group have emerged as a major market for tea; since the mid-1980s their share of world tea imports has exceeded that of the developed market-economies. Over the 1980s, the former Soviet Union had become a fast-growing market for tea, but severe foreign exchange shortage which accompanied the economic reforms after 1990 led to a sharp decline in tea imports in 1991 and 1992–3.

The marketing of tea

Tea has traditionally been sold through public auctions where brokers representing producers sell to buyers (usually other brokers) who put forward the highest bid. This auction system would seem, on the surface, to approximate the perfect market where prices are determined solely by the interplay of supply and demand. However, analysis of the links between selling brokers and firms (many in foreign ownership) operating tea estates, and the small number of buying brokers, has indicated the possibility of some collusion among brokers to influence prices.[7] A Commission of Enquiry into the tea auction system, set up by the Sri Lanka government in the early 1970s, concluded that it appears that there is 'a high degree of collusion that prevails in buying and ... wide scope for collusion between brokers and buyers'.[8] Such collusion, if it occurred, would tend to reduce the price at which producers could sell tea at the auctions, and would also affect prices of direct sales.

The various tea auctions have accounted for several decades for about two-thirds of global sales of tea (see Table 2.8). The major change since 1970 has been a sharp decline in the relative importance of the London auctions, from about 13 per cent of the tea produced in the countries covered by that table to 8 per cent in 1980, and to under 3 per cent in the early 1990s. The switch away from sales at the London auctions has reflected a general belief in producing countries that selling through London carries cost disadvantages for producers. One consideration has been the possibility that where tea exports are taxed on an *ad valorem* basis tea sent to the London

Table 2.8   *Sales of tea at auctions, 1970–1993 (sales in 1000 tonnes, and percentage of production)*

| | Sales at auctions | | | As % of production | |
	London	Producing countries	Total	London	Producing countries
1970	104	556	660	12.7	55.3
1980	89	682	771	8.3	55.2
1985	55	861	916	3.8	66.9
1990	44	919	963	3.0	63.6
1993	29	873	902	1.9	58.2

Note: Auctions in producing countries include those in India, Sri Lanka, Kenya, Bangladesh, Indonesia, and Argentina.

Source: *Annual Bulletin of Statistics* (various issues), International Tea Committee, London.

[7] See in particular, the analysis and discussion of this issue in UNCTAD (1982*a*).
[8] Government of Ceylon (1974), quoted in UNCTAD (1982*a*).

auctions might be undervalued. Moreover, the use of auctions abroad would normally incur foreign exchange costs which would not arise if a local auction centre were used. A third consideration has been the belief that the bargaining strength of sellers at the London auctions is likely to be weaker than in auctions in the country of origin. China—not included in Table 2.8—has in effect bypassed the auction system by selling its tea exports directly to firms in importing countries.

Trends and cycles in auction prices

The relative decline in the London auctions raises the question as to whether London auction prices are still representative of the trend in tea prices worldwide. Though a weighted average of prices at all tea auctions, both in London and in the producing countries, would no doubt be a more accurate guide, the average price recorded at the London auctions remains the generally accepted indicator of world tea prices, and is the price used in the present study.[9]

Average London tea prices have been on a modest downward trend since 1980. From the years 1980–2 to 1990–2, tea prices declined, on average, by 0.5 per cent a year. However, real tea prices (i.e. nominal prices deflated by the movement in manufactures unit value) fell much more sharply over this period, by 4.0 per cent a year. Superimposed on the downward trend have been continual annual fluctuations, with an abnormal price peak in 1984. A similar development had occurred in the 1970s, with a price peak in 1977, and a downward trend in real tea prices of 3.0 per cent a year between 1970–2 and 1980–2.

As mentioned earlier, for the cocoa and coffee markets a close correlation was found between the movement in prices and changes in the ratio of world stocks to world consumption. However, for tea the size of stocks held is relatively small, reflecting their perishability, so that tea stocks function as pipeline stocks rather than as a means of equilibrating

---

[9] The London auction price (average for all tea sold) is not a price in the usual sense of relating to a specific grade, variety, or quality. The trend in this price is thus influenced by shifts in the relative importance of different grades, qualities, etc., as well as by movements in prices *per se*.

world supply and demand by influencing the price. More-over, the available statistics on tea stocks are, in effect, limited to those for the UK, which, as was seen earlier, is a declining market for this beverage. Consequently, it could not be expected that changes in UK's stocks would show a correla-tion with the movement in tea prices as high as the corre-sponding correlations for cocoa and coffee. However, the econometric study described in Chapter 9 succeeded in demonstrating a statistically significant negative relationship between the world tea price and the ratio of UK tea stocks to world tea exports (see that chapter for the detailed results).

Terms of trade gains and losses

Apart from the years 1984–5, when real tea prices were at a peak,[10] tea-exporting countries suffered foreign exchange losses during the 1980s as a result of the deterioration in real tea prices. Over the first half of the 1980s, the unit value of manufactures had fallen below the 1980 level, and this, combined with the higher level of prices in 1984 and 1985, resulted in a substantial terms of trade gain of about $270m. (annual average). However, after 1985 there has been a sub-stantial terms of trade loss, averaging some £450m. a year up to 1993, or almost 30 per cent of the value of tea exports in 1980. As Table 2.9 indicates, the annual rate of loss increased substantially, from $370m. in 1986–8 to $450m. in 1989–91, and to $580m. in 1992–3. About three-fifths of the terms of trade loss during 1986–93 resulted from higher unit values of manufactures, with only two-fifths being due to lower unit values for tea. Over the whole period from 1981 to 1993, the net cumulative loss attributable to the fall in the real price of tea amounted to $2.3bn., or some $175m. a year, equivalent to just over 10 per cent of the value of tea exports in 1980.

For only two major tea-exporting countries, Sri Lanka and Kenya, does tea account for over 20 per cent of total merchan-dise exports; in 1990–1, the proportion was 24 per cent for each country. Over the period 1986 to 1992, the foreign

---

[10] The high level of tea prices in 1984 appears to have been due to a temporary ban on tea exports by India in the 1983–4 season to assure ade-quate supplies to the domestic market at that time.

Table 2.9 *Change in value of tea exports from developing countries in relation to terms of trade effect, 1980–1993 (values in $ bn.)*

	1980	1981–5	1986–8	1989–91	1992–3
Value of tea exports	1.55	1.59	1.41	1.77	1.50
Change from 1980	—	0.04	−0.14	0.22	−0.05
of which:					
Unit value change	—	0.08	−0.21	−0.01	−0.18
Volume change	—	−0.04	0.07	0.23	0.13
Terms of trade effect	—	0.27	−0.37	−0.45	−0.58
As % of 1980 exports	—	18	−24	−29	−37

Note: This table excludes exports from China and Viet Nam.

Sources: as Table 1.1.

exchange loss attributable to the deterioration in the real price of tea averaged about $100m. a year for Sri Lanka (representing almost 30 per cent of the value of tea exports in 1980), while for Kenya the corresponding loss was higher, at some $160m. a year (almost 100 per cent of the 1980 export level).

3

International Remedial Action

Until the end of the 1970s, there had been a broad international consensus in favour of negotiating agreements with economic provisions, where feasible, between commodity producing and consuming countries in order to reduce excessive short-term price fluctuations and, in some cases, to achieve price levels 'remunerative to producers and equitable to consumers'. The vagueness of this objective was deliberate, intending to provide merely a framework within which specific price objectives could be negotiated. For both cocoa and coffee, such international agreements have been negotiated, and renegotiated, over many years, the coffee agreements having begun in 1962, and those for cocoa in 1972.

However, these and other international commodity agreements (ICAs) apart from that for natural rubber, had either lapsed or become non-operative by the beginning of the 1990s. This has reflected three major problems. First, an essentially technical problem arose because each ICA was devoted to achieving a short-term objective (viz. stabilizing temporary price fluctuations), whereas for many commodities, including both cocoa and coffee, the major problem in the 1980s had been the emergence of long-term structural surpluses, with abnormally large stock overhangs. The limited financial resources available for short-term stabilization clearly could not deal effectively with problems of acute structural oversupply.

A second problem arose from a fundamental difference of views between developing producing countries and developed consuming countries on the function of the price range to be defended by an ICA. In periods of falling prices, representatives of consuming countries have argued that the agreed price range should be reduced to accord with the change in market conditions, whereas the producing countries have argued that in such conditions an ICA should be used to support the minimum of the agreed price range. A third problem, particularly in very recent years, has been that the governments of some of the larger consuming countries no longer wish to support the concept of regulation of international commodity markets, even if confined to short-term stabilization, so that they are generally averse to the continuance of the traditional form of ICA.

As a result, it would now appear unlikely that co-operative producer–consumer remedial action will be taken, at least in the short- and medium-term future, to address the problem of persistent depressed levels of commodity prices, without a change in the attitude of consuming countries to the need for market intervention. The immediate question that arises is whether producer countries can themselves devise viable schemes which could raise current depressed levels of prices so as to achieve improved terms of trade and improved levels of export revenues, while achieving a better long-term balance in the market, i.e. by moving towards a position where there are little or no unwanted stocks over-hanging the market, and where a reasonable balance exists between global supply and demand. In principle, these objectives can be attained by some form of supply management scheme.

The successful negotiation of a new International Cocoa Agreement in 1993, however, which is discussed in more detail below, gives rise to some hope that a compromise formula can be evolved whereby a production regulation scheme devised by the producing countries can be operated within the framework of a producer–consumer Agreement. For coffee, by contrast, the recent stalemate in the negotiations for a new Agreement has led the producing countries to devise a scheme to restrict exports by retaining a proportion of their output in domestic stocks. An assessment of these recent policy changes can best be considered against the post-war evolution of international regulatory policy and of international action affecting the markets for tropical beverages.

3.1 THE INTERNATIONAL COCOA AGREEMENTS

The high volatility of world cocoa prices in earlier post-war decades had been a major constraint on the development efforts of producing countries, while the chocolate industry in developed countries—the principal users of cocoa—also had an interest in reducing price instability. Discussions on possible remedial measures between cocoa-producing and-consuming countries began in the mid-1950s under the auspices of FAO, followed by negotiations in the United Nations in the 1960s, culminating in the first International Cocoa Agreement, 1972, negotiated in UNCTAD. Three further Agreements followed, in 1975, 1980, and 1986.

All four of the Agreements stated that their main objectives were:

   (i) to prevent excessive fluctuations in cocoa prices which adversely affect the long-term interests of both producers and consumers; and
  (ii) to achieve a balanced expansion of the world cocoa economy, including the alleviation of serious economic difficulties arising if adjustment between production and consumption cannot be effected by normal market forces alone as rapidly as circumstances require.[1]

In addition, the three earlier Agreements, but not that of 1986, included the objective of stabilizing and increasing the earnings of producing countries from the export of cocoa, so as to provide them with resources for accelerated economic growth and social development, while taking into account the interests of consumers in importing countries.

Each Agreement included a negotiated price range for cocoa, with specified mechanisms for its defence. The first two Agreements provided for an export quota scheme, supported by a buffer stock, with a maximum capacity of 250,000

---

[1] The other elements of the concept of a 'balanced' expansion of the world cocoa economy specified in the Agreements were the securing of an equilibrium in the long term between supply and demand, and the assurance of adequate supplies at reasonable prices, equitable to producers and consumers.

tonnes, to absorb cocoa produced in excess of quotas.[2] However, neither of these Agreements became operative, since in each case the agreed price range was far below the level of market prices. Since market prices remained above the maximum prices specified in the Agreements, the buffer stock could not accumulate cocoa, and nor could it defend the Agreements' ceiling prices.

Under the 1980 Agreement, export quotas were abolished and the buffer stock became the main price-defence mechanism, though its maximum capacity was kept at 250,000 tonnes.[3] The 1986 Agreement again omitted export quotas, and maintained the 250,000 tonnes maximum for the buffer stock. However, as the buffer stock had a carry-over stock of 100,000 tonnes from the previous Agreement, the effective purchasing maximum was reduced to 150,000 tonnes. This Agreement also provided for a withholding scheme, under which a total of 120,000 tonnes could be withheld by producing countries if the physical or financial capacity of the buffer stock was reached.

However, neither the 1980 nor the 1986 Agreement was effective. Under the former, the minimum price was defended in the early months of the Agreement by buffer stock purchases of 100,000 tonnes, but thereafter the sharp appreciation of the US dollar, in which the price range was denominated, prevented sales being made by the buffer stock. The 1986 Agreement changed the price range to one denominated in SDRs to avoid the complications arising from large swings in the value of the dollar. In the first year or so of the Agreement, the buffer stock purchased a further 150,000 tonnes to defend the lower intervention price, thus reaching its maximum capacity of 250,000 tonnes. At this point—at the end of February 1988—no agreement could be reached between producing and consuming countries as to whether the price range should be reduced to bring it more in line with market conditions. This disagreement prevented the introduction of

---

[2] In addition, these agreements provided for the sale for non-traditional uses of cocoa surplus to quotas and to the buffer stock.

[3] Provision was also made for the maximum capacity of the buffer stock to be increased to 350,000 tonnes if the Agreement was extended for more than a year.

the withholding scheme and finally led to the suspension of the price-stabilization provisions of the Agreement. Negotiations for a new cocoa Agreement with economic provisions began in April 1992.

This brief review[4] of the first four Agreements shows that none of them succeeded in achieving their stated objectives, the reasons for this varying from the earlier to the later Agreements. The 1972 and 1975 Agreements were inoperative essentially because the price range to be defended was unrealistically low, and the provisions for revising the price range were inadequate. Under the 1980 Agreement, the buffer stock rapidly exhausted its financial resources, thus losing any control over the market. Clearly, in the absence of export quotas, effective market control would have required a very much larger buffer stock, whereas the size of the buffer stock was maintained at the original level. During the course of the 1986 Agreement, the global surplus of cocoa began its rapid increase—total stocks rising to some 1.5 million tonnes by mid-1991 from 700,000 tonnes in mid-1987—so that buffer stock purchases, at 150 thousand tonnes, had virtually no impact on the market.

A new International Cocoa Agreement with economic provisions was concluded in 1993. A key feature of this Agreement is a production management policy, involving the establishment of a Production Committee to co-ordinate national cocoa policies and programmes, and 'recommend the application of any measures and activities, including where appropriate diversification, likely to help re-establish a lasting equilibrium between world cocoa supply and demand as soon as possible.' The Committee is to 'fix indicative figures for annual levels of global production necessary to achieve and maintain equilibrium between supply and demand in accordance with the aims of the Agreement.' Each producing member country would then draw up a programme for the adjustment of its production in the framework of the production management programme. The Committee will be informed by producers of the results of their

---

[4] More detailed reviews and appraisals of the earlier cocoa Agreements are given in Gordon-Ashworth (1984), UNCTAD (1985), Gilbert (1987), and Maizels (1992).

national programmes, and will then submit reports to the Council of the new Agreement.[5]

The Agreement would not provide for a buffer stock,[6] the levy arrears of some producer countries being offset against their shares of the proceeds from buffer stock sales. The Agreement also includes measures to promote cocoa consumption.

The new cocoa Agreement would appear to constitute an important breakthrough in the stalemate of recent years in regard to the renegotiation of an existing ICA. For the first time, a consensus has been reached in negotiations between producers and consumers on the need for practical measures to raise the price of a commodity in structural surplus.

Moreover, the new Agreement would give priority to the issue of raising depressed price levels over the traditional ICA concern with short-term price stabilization. This is fully in accord with the argument that the dominant feature of the international commodity markets over the past decade has been the persistence of depressed price levels, and that measures to remedy this situation should now receive priority in the formulation of international commodity policy and international action.[7]

3.2   THE INTERNATIONAL COFFEE AGREEMENTS

The large price cycles in the world coffee market, and the associated instability and uncertainty in the coffee export earnings of producing countries, have been the principal incentive in the post-war search for an effective international stabilizing mechanism for this commodity. A series of one-year agreements among producing countries was negotiated in the later 1950s and early 1960s to combat a coffee surplus by regulating exports, but the need for a long-term agreement and for supporting action by importing countries led to nego-

---

[5] UNCTAD (1993).

[6] The International Cocoa Council agreed to liquidate the buffer stock under the 1986 Agreement, and the rules for its liquidation were agreed in September 1993.

[7] See Maizels (1992), ch. 3.

tiations for a full-fledged international agreement.[8] The first International Coffee Agreement, 1962, 'aimed to achieve a reasonable balance between supply and demand on a basis which will assure adequate supplies of coffee to consumers and markets for coffee to producers at equitable prices, and which will bring about long-term equilibrium between production and consumption.'

The 1962 Agreement established a system of export quotas as the principal mechanism to maintain prices within an agreed range, though export quotas were fixed only for 'traditional markets', thus providing an opportunity for producers to increase their shipments to non-quota markets, often for resale to quota markets. Such diverted and resold coffee (known as 'tourist' coffee) put downward pressure on world coffee prices and thus tended to undermine the price-stabilizing objective of the Agreement. However, a system of controls, using certificates of origin, was instituted which greatly reduced the importance of 'tourist' coffee.

A second Agreement was negotiated in 1968 at a time of continuing oversupply of coffee, incorporating several changes designed to make the export quota system more flexible, while making it virtually impossible for countries contributing to overproduction to obtain waivers from export quota obligations. This Agreement also established a Diversification Fund to assist producing countries to divert resources from coffee-growing to other activities in order to enhance their economic position, and to enable coffee growers to increase their income. However, this Fund—to which contributions amounted to $111m. in all—was too small to have any significant impact on the coffee surplus situation, and it was terminated in 1972.[9]

The export quota system established under the 1968 Agreement was itself terminated towards the end of 1972. That year saw a substantial depreciation of the US dollar, in which the Agreement's price targets were denominated, as well as growing inflationary pressures, and large stock changes.

[8] See Vogelvang (1988: ch. 2) for a more detailed discussion of the background to the various coffee Agreements.
[9] For further discussion of the Coffee Diversification Fund see Maizels (1992: 253).

Against this background, producing and consuming countries were not able to agree on how export quotas should be changed. There followed a free-market period until a third Agreement was negotiated to come into force in 1976. However, an unusually severe frost in 1975 in the coffee-growing areas of Brazil resulted in high coffee prices in 1976, and even higher prices in 1977. Since the consuming countries could not agree on high price support levels, the economic clauses of the Agreement were rendered temporarily ineffective. This prompted unilateral action by the main producing countries to co-ordinate export sales, while in 1978 the Latin American producers (the 'Bogotá Group') established a fund to support coffee prices.

This price-support activity was conducted, to a large extent, by operations on the coffee futures markets in London and New York. However, the coffee price boom collapsed in 1978, with substantial losses on the futures contracts of the Bogotà Group. The Group formed a new trading company (Pancafé) in 1980 to help stabilize world coffee prices by buying from producing countries and building its own stocks, as well as trading futures contracts. These market interventions by producers were strongly opposed by the main consuming countries, especially the USA, as being inconsistent with the spirit of the International Coffee Agreement.

Under US pressure, the Bogotá Group agreed to phase out the market activities of Pancafé during 1981, while the USA agreed to help bring back export quotas within the framework of the 1976 Agreement. Quotas were introduced for the first time under that Agreement, in the autumn of 1980.[10] A fourth Agreement, that of 1983, was negotiated to run from October 1983 to September 1989, it being essentially a continuation of the export quota system based on an overall agreed quota for 'traditional markets'. The 1983 Agreement, however, collapsed in July 1989, during a period of oversupply when coffee prices were falling in spite of two successive cuts in the global export quota. The main coffee-consuming countries argued strongly for a reduction in the agreed price range to be defended in the light of the changes in the market

_____

[10] Vogelvang (1988: 58).

situation, whereas the producers wished to restrict supply further in order to safeguard the minimum price of the agreed range.

Apart from this fundamental difference of view concerning the essential functions of an international commodity agreement, there were additional divergencies among the member countries as regards the operation of the coffee Agreement. The main consuming countries argued that two major defects should be corrected. One was that the use of a global export quota, covering all types of coffee, meant that supply had become inflexible and unable to meet adequately the shift in demand in the consuming countries in favour of arabica, and away from robusta, coffee. The other defect for the consumers was that substantial quantities of coffee were being sold at discounted prices to countries not members of the Agreement, which were therefore benefiting at the expense of member countries.

As mentioned in Chapter 2, coffee prices fell sharply after the suspension of export quotas in mid-1989, with large revenue losses for the producing countries. The responses of these countries to the revenue crisis, however, varied very considerably. Some, indeed, such as the Central American countries producing high-quality 'mild' coffee, welcomed the free market situation since they believed that their exports had previously been unduly restrained by export quotas, so that they had been forced to sell substantial proportions of their exports to non-quota markets at heavily discounted prices. Brazil, the largest producer, opposed the reintroduction of export quotas, believing that it could better maintain its market share without them. Other countries, particularly the African robusta coffee producers, were however generally in favour of a rapid return to export regulation. By November 1989, the President of Uganda called for a general 10 per cent cut in coffee production in order to raise prices,[11] but it was not until the summer of 1991 that the Latin American producers—including both Brazil and Colombia—could agree on a plan to withhold 10 per cent of production from the market in order to raise prices of arabica varieties.[12]

[11] *Financial Times*, 21 Nov. 1989.   [12] *Ibid.*, 15 Aug. 1991.

Producer pressure for early action to raise prices, including Brazil's renewed interest in export quotas, was no doubt an important incentive for the consuming countries to give serious consideration to the elements of a new international agreement. A Working Group on International Co-operation on Coffee, established by the International Coffee Council, began consideration of proposals on 'future co-operation on coffee matters' in December 1991, and issued its final report in April 1992. This indicated that a consensus had been reached for the negotiation of a new market-oriented Agreement, based on a universal quota (i.e. an export market with no distinction between member and non-member countries), and supported by an effective system of controls.[13] By October 1992, a definition of the universal quota had been agreed, while the other key elements of a new Agreement were still under negotiation.[14]

Had these negotiations been successful, it was clear that since a new Agreement was to be market-oriented, the consuming countries would not have agreed to a price range above current or prospective free market levels. Thus, the new Agreement under negotiation appeared unlikely to provide the increase in coffee export revenues which producing countries needed to offset at least a substantial proportion of their terms of trade losses.

However, the negotiations for a new Agreement broke down by early 1993, and producing countries began to consider some form of co-operation to improve their earnings in the world coffee market. An agreement among Latin American producing countries was reached in May 1993 under which the Central American producers were to withhold 15 per cent of their production from the export market, while Brazil and Colombia were to limit exports to 17m. and 13m. bags of 60 kg. each, respectively. This agreement was superseded some months later by a wider accord covering both Latin American and African coffee-producing countries,

---

[13] The USA stated that it would participate in a new Agreement with economic clauses only if it was based on a universal quota; market-orientation; an effective control system; and the absence of 'infeasible market interventions' such as buffer stocks or retention schemes (*ibid.*, 7 Apr. 1992).

[14] *Ibid.*, 2 Oct. 1992.

under which these countries agreed to retain up to 20 per cent of their exportable output, and which was to become operative as from October 1993.

Even with a 20 per cent cut target, however, it would seem likely that some producing countries, at least, may find it difficult to meet this target. One problem will be finding adequate financing of the cost of stocking the additional coffee being held off the export market. This could be particularly onerous for most African countries. Policing the scheme may also present many practical difficulties, especially as the consuming countries will not be involved. None the less, to the extent that the scheme is successful in raising prices from depressed levels, it would materially assist in financing additional stocks and thus in firming market 'sentiment' as well.

Moreover, the proposed retention scheme is intended to be flexible, in so far as the full 20 per cent of exportable production would be retained only while the indicator coffee price[15] remained below 75 US cents a lb.; between 75 and 80 cents, only 10 per cent, would be retained, while above 80 cents the retention scheme would be suspended. Producing countries involved in the retention scheme, accounting for about 90 per cent of world exports, have agreed to establish an Association of Coffee Producing Countries, with headquarters in Brazil, to monitor the retention programmes of individual countries, with the assistance of an independent auditor.[16] As a result of the producers' action, the USA announced its withdrawal from the International Coffee Organization.[17] Thus, the co-operative approach to supply management, which emerged in the cocoa negotiations, is in stark contrast to the confrontation between producing and consuming interests which now dominates in the coffee market.

3.3 INTERNATIONAL NEGOTIATIONS ON TEA

The collapse of tea prices during the early 1930s led to the establishment of an International Tea Agreement among

---

[15] The 15-day average of the International Coffee Organization's indicator price for robusta coffee.

[16] *Financial Times*, 23 Sept. 1993.

[17] *Ibid.*, 30 Sept. 1993.

producing countries to support prices at remunerative levels. This agreement, which was based on export quotas, succeeded in maintaining prices at about 75–80 per cent of their pre-Depression level. After the end of the Second World War, however, the Agreement lapsed and has not been renewed.

None the less the downward trend in tea prices during the 1950s and 1960s prompted many producing countries to reconsider the need for international co-operation to halt this trend so as to protect their tea industries and their foreign exchange earnings from tea exports. A meeting of tea-producing countries in 1969, convened to consider the possibilities for international action, reached .an agreement to establish voluntary export quotas for 1970. This informal arrangement had an immediate impact on 'market sentiment' and resulted in a short-term improvement in the level of tea prices. The informal agreement, which was renewed a year later to cover exports in 1971, collapsed however as a result of the opposition of the main African producing countries to any restriction on the expansion of their tea exports. In any case, it seems doubtful whether the voluntary export quotas— which were based essentially on bids by producer country governments—did, in fact, represent a significant cut in the volume of tea coming on the world market.

The issue was taken up again in 1974 in the framework of the FAO where a Working Party was established to review the feasibility of an international agreement on tea to cover, *inter alia*, a minimum export price arrangement, and the co-ordination and regulation of marketing to avoid the accumulation of stocks in importing countries that would have depressing effects on prices.[18] However, neither of these objectives was pursued, and nor was the earlier proposal for market regulation by export quotas, the fundamental problem continuing to be the objections of the governments of Kenya and several other countries with programmes for expansion

[18] Other elements considered by the Working Party were market promotion, including the development of new markets for tea; the rationalization of marketing to achieve the most favourable prices, with special reference to the feasibility of expanding auctions in producing countries; and provisions for an independent market intelligence service for tea-exporting countries.

of tea production to agree to any quantitative limitation on tea exports.

In this connection an interesting proposal made by Sri Lanka, and supported by India, was for a scheme of export regulation based on the 'principle of differential growth'. This principle would have allowed Kenya and other newly established tea-exporting countries to take up the greater part of the growth in world import demand, while the two large traditional tea exporters—India and Sri Lanka—would restrict their export growth to marginal rates. Total tea supply (i.e. the global export quota) would be fixed at an amount designed to yield an agreed level of prices in the world tea market. At a later stage, to be determined by negotiation, the export growth rates of the traditional exporters would be allowed to rise to more normal levels.

This concept of differential growth was proposed in order to accommodate the early phase of the smallholder expansion programmes of the East African tea-producing countries. The latter, however, were not prepared to accept this proposal, since they believed it would restrict the rate of planned development of the smallholder tea industry.[19] None the less, it is a principle which might usefully be reconsidered, where relevant, in a future supply management scheme involving both established and new producing countries.

[19] Part of this development was financed by loans from the World Bank and the Commonwealth Development Corporation.

4

Supply Management Options

The persistence of depressed levels of prices reflects an underlying structural surplus in the world market, a surplus which is the result of a faster rate of expansion of productive capacity (and of production) than of consumption. This has been the experience in many markets, both of primary commodities and of manufactured goods. Where structural surpluses have arisen in developed countries, governments have typically resorted to mechanisms involving some form of supply management designed to support producer incomes above a minimum level. Such support mechanisms have been widespread in regard to temperate-zone agriculture, but they have been used also for industries such as shipbuilding, steel, and textiles.

Surpluses in the markets for primary commodities of export interest to developing countries have generally been treated as reflecting one phase of a longer economic cycle, particularly for tree crops with a long gestation period. For such commodities, excess supply in one phase is generally balanced by excess demand subsequently, which forms the rational basis for the operation of an international buffer stock, or a scheme of export regulation, or both, to mitigate the rise in prices in a phase of excess demand, and the fall in prices when there is excess supply. However, as already mentioned, in recent years the larger developed countries have objected to the use of export regulation as an instrument for mitigating short-term fluctuations in the prices of commodities subject to international commodity agreements. Their objections to the regulation of export supply have remained even stronger when the aim of an international agreement was to raise market prices, even from persistently depressed levels, rather than merely to smooth out short-term price fluctuations.

It may be, however, that the successful conclusion of the new cocoa agreement in 1993, mentioned in Chapter 3, reflects a shift in policy stance by the major developed countries in so far as this agreement gives priority to measures designed to achieve a better balance in the cocoa market by reducing the growth of cocoa production, thus tending to raise the level of cocoa prices. However, the breakdown in the negotiations for a new coffee agreement, to which reference was also made in Chapter 3, does not augur well for the emergence of a common approach by consuming and producing countries to meeting the problems of structural oversupply by appropriate supply management schemes.

Since the developed countries are also by far the largest consumers of the tropical beverages, it would be important for any supply management scheme for these beverage crops operated by producing countries to take the interests of consumers fully into account. Thus, the scheme should not be envisaged as a cartel, aiming to raise prices to 'what the market will bear', but rather its price objective should be the more pragmatic and realistic one of achieving a level of prices, in real terms, somewhere between present depressed levels and, say, the levels which existed in the early 1980s. Where exactly that level should be would be a matter for further consideration and negotiation.

Though such a scheme, where feasible and viable, would bring clear benefits to producing countries in terms of foreign exchange earnings, it would also benefit the developed consuming countries, particularly if its objectives also included the reduction of short-term price fluctuations. An increase in the level of foreign exchange earnings of producing countries would inevitably result in a corresponding expansion in purchases by these countries of capital goods and other essentials from the developed countries, thus helping to strengthen the export sector of the latter countries. Moreover, a greater stability of market prices, combined with more remunerative price levels, would contribute to avoiding a damaging contraction in productive capacity which would otherwise occur, thus safeguarding consumers' interests if demand for the commodity were to expand in a future period.

Consumers' interests would in any case be safeguarded if a supply management scheme were operated within the framework of an international commodity agreement embracing both consumers and producers, as is now the case for cocoa. But even a producer-only scheme, such as the retention scheme for coffee, should not evoke adverse consumer reactions if it had relatively modest price-raising objectives. Moreover, a producer-only scheme could also be regarded as preparing the way for a later producer–consumer agreement once a reasonable long-term balance in the market has been achieved.

4.1 ALTERNATIVE APPROACHES TO SUPPLY MANAGEMENT

Several possible approaches to evolving a supply management scheme for the tropical beverages are considered in this study, though not every alternative is discussed for each beverage because some would not be suitable for the particular conditions of each beverage market. The alternatives, which are not necessarily mutually exclusive, are:

   (i) a stock reduction scheme;
  (ii) an export quota scheme;
 (iii) a production reduction scheme;
 (iv) the imposition of a uniform *ad valorem* export tax.

A stock reduction scheme

The specific objective here is gradually to reduce an abnormally high stock overhang in an orderly manner, thus avoiding serious structural dislocation in the commodity economy concerned, while allowing the price mechanism to continue to function freely. Since there is no specific price objective it should, in principle, be easier to negotiate a stock reduction scheme than, say, an export quota arrangement based on a pre-agreed price range to be defended. The feasibility of devising a workable stock reduction scheme for either cocoa or coffee—both of which have large stock overhangs—derives considerable credibility from the experience in recent years of the supply rationalization scheme implemented by the Association of Tin Producing Countries (ATPC), since the stock overhang problems of tin and of cocoa and coffee bear marked similarities. Stocks of tin had been building up over the first half of the 1980s, as a result of a decline in consumption combined with growing output. By October 1985, when the International Tin Agreement collapsed, world tin stocks (excluding normal working stocks) amounted to some 80,000 tonnes, equivalent to almost five months' world consumption. Prices on the London Metal Exchange, which had averaged almost $12,000 a tonne, collapsed to $5,700 (by over 50 per cent) by the second half of 1986.

A supply rationalization scheme was adopted by member countries of the ATPC, designed to reduce the stock overhang by limiting exports to below the forecast level of demand. The two main non-member producing countries (Brazil and China) agreed to co-operate by limiting their tin exports also. The scheme, which involved agreement on 'export entitlements' for individual producing countries, began in March 1987, and has since been renewed on an annual basis. By the spring of 1989, the stock overhang had been reduced to under 40,000 tonnes, though it rose somewhat to about 45,000 tonnes in 1990–1. The stock reduction appears to have been an important factor in strengthening market sentiment and expectations of a price recovery. Prices did in fact rise to about $7,200 per tonne, on average, in 1988 and to $8,670 per tonne in 1989. Since then, tin prices declined once again, to about $5,500 per tonne, by the end of 1991, and to $4,775 by the end of 1993, causing many tin-mines to go out of production, before recovering somewhat to $6,285 by the end of 1995.

An export quota scheme

The essential difference between a traditional export quota scheme and one based on export entitlements to reduce a large stock overhang is that the former is specifically related to the achievement of an agreed price objective, while the latter influences prices indirectly by improving market sentiment, promoting confidence that prices are likely to improve with the reduction in stocks.

There is a double negotiation involved in an export quota scheme; first, an agreement has to be reached on a price objective, and then negotiation is necessary to allocate a global export quota (believed to be that amount which would achieve the price objective) among the various producing countries. Thus, these negotiations are likely to be much more complex and time-consuming than that for a stock reduction scheme, though if only producing countries were involved, the difficulties of reaching an agreement on a price objective would be considerably less than if consuming countries were also involved.

There are a number of well-known problems arising from export quota schemes, which a supply management scheme of this type would need to take into account. One important problem is how best to ensure that the quotas are subject to change to allow appropriately for changes in comparative advantage. Another problem is how best to attract all actual or potential major suppliers to join the scheme, to avoid it being undermined by increased exports from non-members. As regards ensuring flexibility in the allocation of export quotas (while avoiding major disputes on this issue among exporting countries), it would facilitate the operation of a quota regime if some appropriate indicator of the need for revision of quotas could be agreed, combining, for example, recent export performance, current levels of stocks, and the importance of the commodity in the exports of individual countries. As regards accommodating the interests of potential major suppliers, some compromise will need to be found between the interests of established exporters and those of new and growing exporting countries, perhaps by allowing the latter to have progressively larger market shares.[1]

A production reduction scheme

An alternative approach to the regulation of exports would be an agreement among producing countries to cut their levels of production for a specified period. This could be done by

[1] These problems are discussed in greater detail in Maizels (1992: 82–4). See also the reference at the end of Ch. 3 to the quota allocation principles proposed for tea.

reaching agreement on the global reduction in supplies over, say, the coming five years that appeared necessary, taking into account the probable degree of overproduction and surplus stocks that would accrue in the absence of market regulation, and then allocating the global reduction among individual producing countries, e.g. on the basis of their actual production levels in the recent past.[2]

For cocoa, for which exports account for the great bulk of production (85 per cent in 1988–90), a production regulation arrangement is likely to have a very similar outcome to an export quota scheme of equal restrictive effect, but for coffee and tea, where the export share of production is appreciably lower (74 per cent for coffee and 54 per cent for tea in 1988–90), the effects on world market prices can differ considerably, depending on the extent to which domestic stocks can be drawn upon to maintain exports.

A production reduction scheme does have an advantage over an export quota, however, in so far as it is based on a uniform percentage cut in current, or recent, levels of production. Since this would leave the relative production levels of the various producing countries unchanged, it should not give rise to major disputes about market shares—a common difficulty in negotiations on export quotas. However, there may well be problems in the operation of a production regulation agreement owing to lack of adequate or reliable statistics of crop outturn in various countries. Moreover, in a situation of very large stock overhang, such as existed for cocoa and coffee in the later 1980s, a cut in production can readily be met by drawing down stocks, at least in some countries, so as to maintain the existing level of exports. This would clearly be contrary to the intention of a production reduction scheme, so that it would not occur for political reasons or, if it did occur, it would quickly undermine the scheme itself.

A uniform ad valorem export tax

A quite different approach, aiming to raise depressed levels of export revenues, would be the imposition of a uniform *ad*

[2] This is the approach adopted in the new cocoa Agreement (see Ch. 3.1).

valorem tax on exports from all (or all the main) producing countries. It would be essential to cover a high proportion of available, or potentially available, supply since otherwise the importing countries could switch their purchases to countries which have no such tax.

One advantage of this approach would be that this scheme should also be easier to negotiate than an export quota scheme (involving market share allocations), since an export tax, being at a uniform rate, would not discriminate as between different producing countries, so that it would not affect their relative costs or relative selling prices. It could, however, affect their relative gain in export earnings to the extent that their short-term price-elasticities of supply differ significantly.

A big disadvantage of the tax approach, however, as will be shown later, is that a relatively large rate of tax would be required in the case of a tropical beverage, to achieve the same increase in export revenue that would be obtained by a relatively small reduction in supply, a result which is discussed in more detail in later chapters. Another disadvantage of an export tax is likely to arise in the case of an exporting country which has a relatively large domestic market for the commodity in question. Though the tax will raise the total export revenue of all producing countries, the export revenue of a country with a large domestic consumption will rise by less than the average, or could even decline, if the tax is accompanied by a diversion of some potential exports to the domestic market. This case is discussed further in Chapter 5 in relation to Indian exports and consumption of tea.[3]

4.2   OTHER POSSIBLE MECHANISMS

While the four alternatives discussed briefly above would seem to be the most viable, technically, to achieve a substan-

---

[3] A further disadvantage would arise if the main producing countries fixed the prices paid to producers without regard to the export tax, since in this case output would not necessarily fall following the imposition of the tax. However, for all three beverage crops, it was found that the producer price and the export price were significantly related for most countries.

tial expansion in real foreign exchange earnings from exports of tropical beverages, other measures have also been advocated from time to time.

Cocoa. The most recent proposal to raise the depressed level of cocoa prices[4] was a package of measures including:

(i) the creation of a network of national cocoa stocks managed by a central authority representing the producer countries;

(ii) halting the expansion of cocoa cultivation until prices recovered sufficiently, the suggested level being the median price of the International Cocoa Agreement ($2,266 per tonne); and

(iii) a joint producer–consumer programme for disposal of stocks, e.g. sales for animal feed.

There are some problems arising with each of these proposals. If national stocks are to be accumulated, a limit would be set by available government finance, and it seems unlikely that more than a small proportion of the total cocoa stock overhang could have been absorbed in this way. Halting the expansion in cocoa cultivation would be a sensible move on a global basis, but might well require difficult negotiations, since some countries (e.g. Indonesia and Malaysia) had existing expansion programmes in place. In any event, halting expansion (in the sense of the *area* cultivated) would not necessarily halt the expansion in production. Finally, sales for non-food uses, or non-human consumption, are unlikely by themselves to make a major contribution to reducing the existing stock overhang, though such sales might be a useful complement to export quotas or other mechanisms discussed earlier.

Coffee. The coffee retention scheme referred to earlier is, in some ways, similar to an export quota arrangement. Both would, if successful, result in a cut-back from the level of exports that would otherwise obtain. But the effect of a retention scheme on exports would not necessarily be straightforward to assess, since much would depend on the extent to

---

[4] By a Minister in the Malaysian government: proposal put forward informally at a Conference in Kuala Lumpur (*Financial Times*, 1 Oct. 1991)

which production levels themselves were rising or falling. Moreover, where neither coffee farmers nor their governments could adequately finance additional stocks, there might in some producing countries be pressure to maintain exports at previous levels. A further problem with a production retention scheme is that it would be more difficult to police than a straightforward export quota, since statistics of retained stocks are likely to be deficient in many producing countries.

None the less, the probable impact of the coffee retention scheme operated since 1993 by the coffee-producing countries—which was commenced after the coffee supply management simulations of the present study had been completed— may approximate to that of one of the simulations for an export quota presented in the next chapter.

Tea. It was mentioned earlier that an FAO Working Party had considered the feasibility of introducing a minimum export price arrangement, while in 1982 governments were considering, *inter alia*, the possibility of minimum quality standards for tea.[5] If a quality control could indeed be introduced, it was thought that this would have two major effects:[6] it could lead to more consumer satisfaction with tea and thereby influence demand; and it could remove substandard tea from the export market.

More recently, Indian tea interests have stressed the need for an export quota agreement to stabilize volatile tea prices or in the absence of such an agreement, 'the next best thing would be to have an agreement to export only quality teas.'[7]

However, a major difficulty with the minimum quality proposal is that if quality is measured by price, anomalies will result, since a low price is not necessarily an indicator of poor quality. A number of producing countries—including India, Sri Lanka, and Kenya—have, however, established minimum standards[8] below which teas are destroyed, but the large exporters of low-priced teas—including Argentina,

---

[5] UNCTAD (1982*b*)

[6] UNCTAD (1982*c*), para. 46.

[7] Statement by the Chairman of the Indian Tea Association (*Financial Times*, 23 Apr. 1987).

[8] Based on the International Organization for Standardization (ISO) standard for tea approved in 1977.

China, and Malawi—have not. Since the latter are likely to oppose a ban on the export of either low-priced or low-quality teas, it would seem that the more promising avenue for raising tea quality in the world market would be for importing, rather than exporting, countries to impose uniform minimum standards.

Another possible approach to supply management might be, in principle, an agreement to reduce tea production by a given percentage from, say, the average level of recent years. However, this would not be a viable approach because, unlike coffee and cocoa, the predominant producer, India, is also the largest single market for tea consumption, a market, moreover, which has been growing rapidly.[9] Hence, a cut in Indian tea output is almost certain to result in reduced supplies for export and, consequently, in a lower share of the world tea market, a result which is not likely to be acceptable.

A further approach—proposed in the case of cocoa—was a stock reduction scheme. This would, however, be inappropriate for tea, the quality of which begins to deteriorate after four to five months of storage, so that stocks are normally small in relation to consumption.

---

[9] Domestic tea consumption in India rose by over 150,000 tonnes (45%) from 1980 to 1990, whereas Indian tea exports fell by some 20,000 tonnes (10%) over the same period. These divergent trends continued in the early 1990s.

5

Supply Management Simulations

An assessment of the impact of each of the alternative supply management approaches described in Chapter 4 on the markets for the tropical beverages can best be made by simulations based on computable econometric models. For each beverage, a new model has been constructed from regression equations for production and consumption in each major country involved, together with equations linking the world price to the domestic producer price. For the cocoa model, thirty-nine endogenous variables have been used; for coffee, the model includes fifty-two endogenous variables, while for tea there are forty-two. The model calculation aimed to cover the period from 1963 to 1990 or 1991, though for many of the variables shorter periods had to be used owing to lack of relevant statistics for the 1960s. The full models are set out in Part II.

The simulations generally relate to the second half of the 1980s, since that was the period of sharp deterioration in real prices and real export earnings. The focus is thus on exports of producer countries in terms of their capacity to purchase imports (of manufactured goods), since this emphasizes the key role of exports in commodity-dependent developing countries in providing a dynamic impulse for economic growth or, when real exports are declining, an impulse for economic contraction.[1] For this period, the dynamic simulation results for each of the econometric models were highly

---

[1] The present study does not cover the welfare effects of supply management—defined as producer and consumer surpluses plus the change in government revenue—since these effects are essentially static once-and-for-all gains or losses, whereas the export revenue effects are essentially dynamic, operating via the impact on imports and domestic investment. A recent demonstration that export revenues of developing countries have a dynamic influence on economic growth through their impact on imports (rather than through their impact on productivity in domestic production) is given in Esfahani (1991).

Table 5.1 *Correlations between actual values and model dynamic simulation results*

	World production	World consumption	World stocks	World price
Cocoa (1985–90)	0.98	0.85	0.99	0.97
Coffee (1983–90)	0.95	0.88	0.99/0.25	0.82
Tea (1986–90)	n.a.	n.a.	n.a.	0.76

Note: The coefficient for world coffee production relates to exports of coffee-producing countries members of ICO, that for world coffee consumption relates to ICO members, while the two coefficients for world stocks relate respectively, to producing and consuming ICO members.

correlated with actual out-turn, except for coffee stocks in consuming countries (see Table 5.1), which gives considerable credence to the simulations for the alternative supply management schemes.

Simulations of the effect of each of the selected supply management options proposed in the previous chapter can now be made on the basis of specific assumptions concerning the magnitude of the policy change assumed. Since different assumptions would appear relevant for the different beverage crops, the simulation results for each crop are considered separately here.

5.1 COCOA

For cocoa, the specific assumptions made are set out in Table 5.2. It was assumed, for example, that total cocoa stocks, which had risen sharply after 1985, were cut by 100,000 tonnes, progressively, up to 1990, in which year the assumed level of stocks would have been 600,000 tonnes lower.[2] Since stocks in October 1985 were 522,000 tonnes, rising to 1.4m. tonnes by October 1990, the assumed cuts represented some 20 per cent of 1985 stocks, rising to over 40 per cent of 1990 stocks.

---

[2] In all cases, the assumed cut is not from the actual level in a given year, but from the 'base case' level in that year, i.e. the level derived from the model on the assumption of no supply management policy.

Table 5.2 *Assumptions made for alternative supply management schemes for cocoa*

	Assumption
Stock reduction	Total cocoa stocks assumed to be cut by 100,000 tonnes a year, progressively
Production cut	(a) *Smaller cut*: to achieve a price target in real terms (at 1985 prices) midway between actual 1980 and 1990 prices (b) *Larger cut*: to maintain the 1985 price in real terms up to 1990
Uniform *ad valorem* export tax	Tax rate rising from 10% in 1985 to 35% in 1990, with mean rate over the period of 22.5%.

Two levels of production cuts were also assumed as possible alternative policies. The smaller cut was based on the production level required to achieve a real cocoa price midway between the actual prices of 1980 and 1990. This would seem to be a rather modest price objective, and should have been, in principle, acceptable to consumers. The larger production cut was required to maintain the 1985 level of cocoa prices in real terms in each year up to 1990—a more ambitious objective, since the 1985 real price was very close to that for 1980. Since the great bulk of cocoa production is exported, it was not necessary to include exports, in addition to production, in the model (see Chapter 7), so that no separate simulations for export quotas were made. Finally, for the export tax option it was assumed that a new *ad valorem* export tax had been imposed by all cocoa-producing countries, rising from 10 per cent in 1985 to 35 per cent in 1990.

These particular assumptions are, of course, purely illustrative; different assumptions would yield different results in terms of world prices and export earnings (as well as production, consumption, and stocks). But they do indicate the orders of magnitude of the impact which different supply management schemes would have had in the critical years for the world cocoa market after the mid-1980s.

The effects of each simulated policy change is evaluated by comparing the cocoa model's solution for that change with the solution for the 'base case' of no policy change. The

Table 5.3 *Summary of simulation results for alternative cocoa schemes: annual averages for 1985–1990 (production, consumption and stocks in million tonnes, price in $ per tonne, export earnings in $ bn., simulation results in percentage change from base case.)*

	Produc- tion	Consump- tion	Stocks	Price	Export earnings
Base case (no supply management)	2.12	1.85	0.94	2,304	3.90
Supply management: 1. Stock reduction	−8.4	−4.2	−37	+81	+66
2. Production cut: (a) Smaller cut	−7.0	−0.5	−27	+27	+20
(b) Larger cut	−8.5	−1.8	−35	+52	+40
3. Uniform *ad valorem* export tax	−3.1	−0.5	−13	+12	+9

Note: See Table 5.2 for assumptions made for each simulation.

comparison cannot be with the actual values of cocoa prices, exports, production, and other variables in each year, since these are influenced in part by factors (such as weather variation, unrecorded stock changes, etc.) which were not covered by the model. These omitted variables correspond to the error terms in the equations which influence the determination of market prices through the interaction of world supply and demand.

The simulation results are given in detail in the Statistical Appendix. Here it suffices to focus on the main results. Table 5.3 shows the average annual change over the simulation period in cocoa production, consumption, stocks, price, and export earnings for each supply management option, compared with the base case, while the annual simulations are depicted in Figure 5.1 for export revenue only (since that is the key outcome of a supply management policy).

A stock reduction scheme

The reduction in world cocoa stocks by a target amount can be achieved by some or all of the producer countries restrict-

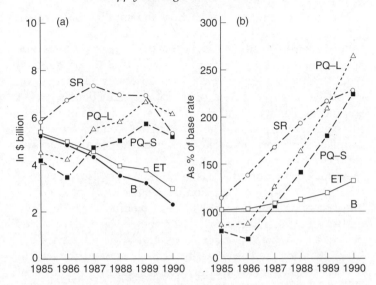

Fig. 5.1 Cocoa: impact of alternative supply management schemes on export revenues, 1985–90.

Note: SR=stock reduction; PQ–S and PQ–L=production quota, smaller cut-back and larger cut-back respectively; ET=export tax; B=base case
Source: Appendix Table B.1.

ing exports, though the total cut in exports will not in general be equal to the reduction in stocks. The higher market prices will reduce demand so that some of the current production will be added into stocks; for example, a fall in supply of 100,000 tonnes could cause a fall in demand of 50,000 tonnes at the higher price, thus reducing stock levels by 50,000 tonnes. The model can be solved to find the production cut-back that reduces stock levels by a target amount. If all producers agreed to join the scheme, and negotiated their shares of export entitlements successfully, then supply would be entirely exogenous. A more realistic case is one where the smaller producers do not join the scheme and so remain endogenous. The higher price induced by the scheme would encourage them to increase their production in both the short and longer run. The parts of the co-operating block would then become the exogenous variable.

The model assumes that each of the supply management schemes is operated jointly by the seven major producers, viz Côte d'Ivoire, Brazil, Malaysia, Ghana, Nigeria, Cameroon, and Indonesia. A reduction in stocks (or in production) would result in higher world cocoa prices, but the effect on export earnings would be offset by the reduction in export shipments. For the smaller producers, assumed not to be in the scheme, there would be a clear gain from higher prices, coupled with any induced increment in production and exports.

A stock reduction of 100,000 tonnes a year, progressively, over the simulation period would have allowed a gradual rise in cocoa stocks, so that by 1990 stocks would have been about midway between the actual 1985 and 1990 levels. For the period as a whole, average stock levels would have been lower than for the base case by 37 per cent, and this would have been associated with an average price of 81 per cent above the base case of no-supply management, and a corresponding increase of 66 per cent in export earnings (see Table 5.3).

The progressive reduction in stocks relative to the base case lifts the world cocoa price, but the model shows a peak in the nominal price, and in export earnings, until 1987 under this stock reduction scheme, and some further widening of the gap between the simulated and the base case price, and export earnings, in later years (see Figure. 5.1).

The model indicates that to achieve a progressive reduction in stocks by 100,000 tonnes a year would have required a slowly increasing production cut relative to the base case. In 1985, for example, the production cut would be 112,000 tonnes, while by 1990 the corresponding cut must be 207,000 tonnes. Lagged responses result in production cuts to achieve the stock reduction target as well as to offset the decline in cocoa consumption induced by the higher price.

A production-cut scheme

The price objective here is to stabilize the world cocoa price in real terms from 1985 to 1990. Two alternative price targets are considered for 1985, the first year of the simulations. The first target is a nominal price midway between the 1980 and the 1990 actual prices ($2,202 per tonne), while the second takes the actual 1985 price ($2,629 per tonne) as the target, so that the former target involves a smaller cut in production than the latter. The reason for taking such a high price for the second alternative is that the mid-decade price—taken for the first alternative—is below the 1985 actual price, so that a simulation based on such a target will predict export levels substantially above those which actually took place. It is difficult to see how such an increase could in practice have been met, and it is likely that the price target would not have been achieved in the first year. Hence a scheme with a higher target price is evaluated which is managed—as for the stock reduction scheme—by agreed production cut-backs.

For each scheme, the price target for each year 1986 to 1990 is the 1985 target adjusted for the rise in unit value of exports of manufactures from developed countries. By 1990, the target nominal price becomes $3,458 per tonne for the first alternative, and $4,127 for the second.

In assessing the simulation results for the period 1985–90 (Table 5.3), it is important to remember that the appropriate comparison is between the simulated values under the price target scheme and the simulated values in the 'no-policy' scheme (base case). The target price is such under each price objective that the simulated price movement is entirely in the opposite direction to the (falling) price in the base case for the whole six-year period. The impact on production under either price target is to require a very substantial cut-back in 1986 after a year in which an increase in production would have been needed to meet the price objective. World consumption is gradually pushed below that in the base case, while after 1987 world stocks are held almost constant by the real constant price objective. For the higher real price objective, world production and world consumption are both slightly lower than under the first scheme.

Cocoa export earnings, as simulated by the model, would have risen substantially above the base case values after 1987 (Figure 5.1), and by 1990 would have been 2–2.5 times the corresponding base case. For the six-year simulation period as a whole, cocoa export earnings would have risen to 20 per cent above the base case, for the smaller export cut-back, and to 40 per cent above, on the larger cut-back.

A *uniform* ad valorem *export tax*

It is assumed that a uniform tax on exports is imposed simultaneously by each of the seven major producing countries. The producer price including tax is determined by the world cocoa price and the exchange rate between US dollars and the local currency. The price received by farmers, which influences area planted and the amount harvested, is this price excluding the tax. This has the effect of attenuating the link between producers and consumers. The total effect on the world price will depend on the structure of the whole model, in which both demand and supply elasticities will be important. The dynamics of farming will also be involved, since decisions to plant less or produce less are now left to economic incentives. In the previous two policy options it was assumed that the government was able to attain the required production or export cut-backs immediately.

For illustrative purposes, the tax rate has been set at 10 per cent in 1985, with increases of 5 percentage points a year until 1990 when the tax reaches 35 per cent A summary of the effects of the tax on the major variables is included in Table 5.3 and Figure 5.1. The simulations indicate that the impact of the gradually increasing export tax is to raise world prices above the base line case by increasing amounts each year. Part of this effect is due to the increases in the tax rate and part is due to the lagged response of production to lower prices, and consumption to the higher prices, brought about by the tax. However, in contrast to the simulated impact of the assumed production cuts on the world cocoa price, the effect of the export tax would be a downward trend in the world price, though at a somewhat higher level than for the base case.

The fall in production induced by the export tax becomes quite strong by the end of the simulation period as planting decisions begin to affect output. By 1990, cocoa production is simulated at about 7 per cent below the base case level, whereas the average reduction over the simulation period as a whole is only 3 per cent. The impact on cocoa consumption is, however, very slight, and because of the low price-elasticity of demand much of the adjustment in the market comes from stock run-down.

The effect of the export tax on the world cocoa price is to raise the average price over the simulation period to $2,570 per tonne, or 12 per cent above the base case level—a much smaller increase than for the stock reduction and production-cut schemes. Similarly, as regards export earnings, the assumed level of export tax would yield a considerably smaller increase over the base level than would the alternative schemes.

Country export earnings

Since the supply side of the cocoa model is built up from output and area equations for each of the seven principal producing countries, the model can be used not only to simulate total supply effects but also the effects on individual producing countries on given assumptions about market shares.

Normally, one can assume that each country would maintain, under a supply management simulation, its average market share that obtained over the simulation period as a whole. However, in the case of cocoa two new producers—Malaysia and Indonesia—were diversifying into cocoa and increasing their production rapidly towards the end of the 1980s, while Ghana, which had suffered a considerable contraction in output in the mid-1980s, was recovering at a fast rate in later years. These three countries accounted for 17 per cent of world cocoa production in 1985, but for 27 per cent in 1990, and were the major part of *incremental* supply during the simulation period. The rapid growth suggests that these countries envisaged substantial gains from producing cocoa and hence would be the most resistant to limitations on exports. In particular, fixing shares of the total production cut-back on the basis of 1985 outputs, or even to the annual averages for 1985–90, would be seen to have had an unfair adverse effect on their production (versus the free market outcome) by 1990.

One possible compromise—which is adopted here—is to take market shares of the seven largest producers (Côte d'Ivoire, Brazil, Ghana, Malaysia, Nigeria, Cameroon, and Indonesia) of their own total production in 1988 as the basis for sharing export entitlements of the target figure. Hence, if Brazil had produced 20 per cent of the output of these seven in 1988, it is assumed that Brazil would be allocated 20 per cent of whatever target production, together with endogenous production of the smaller producing countries, would produce a stock decline of 100,000 tonnes each year from 1985 to 1990.

This is, of course, only one of many possible outcomes for individual producing countries, and the results must thus be taken as a purely illustrative exercise. In an actual negotiation market shares would have to be related to production (or exports) in a very recent period. For example, if the actual shares of production during 1989–92 were taken as the basis, both Indonesia and Ghana would have significantly higher shares than indicated by the 1988 figures, while Brazil in particular would have a significantly lower percentage.

On the basis of the 1988 shares, the impact of the alternative supply management schemes on export earnings is summarized in Table 5.4. The results show that each major producing country would gain from any of the alternative schemes—the only exceptions are losses attributed to Ghana on the

Table 5.4 *Simulated export earnings of major cocoa-producing countries for alternative supply management schemes: 1985–1990 (base case in $ m., other figures in percentage increase over base case.)*

	Base case	Stock reduction	Production cut-back		Export tax
			Smaller	Larger	
Côte d'Ivoire	1,400	72	24	45	11
Brazil	810	70	23	44	10
Ghana	585	15	−17	−2	7
Malaysia	430	87	35	58	2
Nigeria	305	77	28	49	8
Cameroon	265	77	28	49	12
Indonesia	105	102	46	70	18

Note: Figures are annual averages for simulation period.

production-cut alternatives, reflecting essentially its low 1988 share of cocoa production. An alternative simulation, based on production in the early 1990s, would show export earnings gains for all the major cocoa-producing countries.

5.2 COFFEE

The new model of the world coffee market gave a reasonably good fit to the actual values of the relevant variables over the period from 1983 to 1990 (see Table 5.1). This was in spite of the fact that, as discussed in further detail in Part II, the output equations were not very close fits (unlike those for cocoa), while the price variables generally were found to be insignificant in their impact on output in the short term. There was a longer-run effect of prices through the invest-ment decision, but for the simulation period little impact would be expected of prices on supply. The main reason for the less good fit appears to be the increased sensitivity of coffee to climate conditions and the variability of these con-ditions. Such factors are not easy to model and present a dilemma for simulation. In attempting to evaluate an alter-native past history, the weather should be held constant or else it will not be possible to attribute changes to the altered policy variable. Since working with predicted output would mean ignoring special weather factors, in the light of their importance and the lack of sensitivity of output to prices, it was decided to treat production as exogenous so that actual values are used in the 'policy-off' (or base) case.

Making this adjustment to the complete model a set of dynamic simulations for the period 1983 to 1990 was con-structed. The model is linked period by period not only by the obvious impact of lagged prices, but also through the stock level variables. The closing stocks of one period become the opening stocks of the next—hence errors in stocks (which are crucial in price determination) are cumulated forward.

A particular problem arising in the construction of the coffee model was that export quotas had been in force in some years, but not in others. As explained in more detail in Chapter 8, had the quotas prevented world prices from arbitraging to local producer prices, it would have been necessary to take explicit account of the quota levels. However, a statistical test using a dummy variable for the quota years in the country regressions (with the producer price as dependent variable) showed that in no case was the dummy variable significant, a result which allowed a single model to be used for the whole period.

The simulations generally relate to eight major coffee-producing countries which are members of the International Coffee Organization (ICO)—viz. Brazil, Colombia, Mexico, and Guatemala in Latin America, Côte d'Ivoire and Uganda in Africa, and Indonesia and India in Asia—which together account for about two-thirds of total coffee production in ICO member countries. The list of countries was restricted to those for which adequate data series existed for the period 1967 to 1990, on which the econometric calculations were based. (A full discussion of the model can be found in Chapter 8.)

The specific assumptions made for the simulations are set out in Table 5.5. Two levels of production cut-backs are taken as possible alternative supply management policies: the smaller cut-back of 5 per cent from the actual production level in each year, and the larger one of 10 per cent in each year. It was assumed that in each case the cut would be applied by the eight producing countries listed above, while output in other countries was taken as unchanged. For the export quota

Table 5.5 *Assumptions made for alternative supply management schemes for coffee*

	Assumption
1. Production cut	(a) *Smaller cut*: production cut by 5% a year by the eight principal producing countries.
	(b) *Larger cut*: production cut by 10% a year by the eight principal producing countries
2. Export quota	(a) *Smaller cut*: to maintain the mid-point of the price range of 1983 Agreement (130 cents per lb.) constant in real terms.
	(b) *Larger cut*: to maintain price in real terms at 15% above (a), i.e. at 150 cents per lb. at 1983 prices.

option, two levels of export cut-backs were also assumed: the smaller would hold the real price constant from 1983 at 130 cents per lb., while the larger cut-back would support a price 15 per cent higher, i.e. at 150 cents per lb. at 1983 prices. These opening prices in 1983 are increased each year in proportion to the rise in the UN index of unit values of manufactures exported by developed countries. By 1990, the corresponding price targets are then 197 cents per lb. (for the smaller cut-back) and 228 cents per lb. (for the larger).

A third possible supply management approach, the imposition of a uniform *ad valorem* export tax, was also explored. However, for the proposal to benefit producers as well as producer governments, it is necessary that there is some short-term supply response to the change in prices received. With no supply response, the export tax merely lowers prices to farmers by the full amount of the tax while keeping the world price constant. This leaves demand unchanged as would be required to match the unchanged supply. Hence, the full effect of such a tax would be for farmers to lose an amount of revenue proportional to the tax, i.e. if the tax were 10 per cent of the price sold at export, then the farmer would lose 10 per cent of the export value. With unchanged production, the revenue loss in percentage terms (relative to the base case) would be equal to the increase in tax rates.

Such an extreme result makes the export tax unattractive as a policy mechanism when the supply elasticity is extremely low. As explained later (see Chapter 8), for all countries except Brazil and Côte d'Ivoire there is no evidence of significant short-term price-elasticities of output. Only after enough time elapses for the impact on the area harvested to be felt is there a relation between prices and output. Even for Brazil the model found only a very low price-elasticity of output. The two previous policy simulations have reflected this situation by treating output as exogenous over the short to medium term. Accordingly, the export tax would not be an interesting option for coffee-producing countries anxious to raise export revenues and producers' incomes. The remainder of this chapter is therefore confined to summarizing the results of the simulations of the two other policy options mentioned earlier.

A production-cut scheme

The simulation of the 5 per cent cut-back in production shows a very interesting pattern of response. Initially the production-cut of about 3m. bags of coffee is largely met by running down producer stocks. The ratio of stocks to production is thus only slightly disturbed and price rises slightly above the base case. Consumption shows virtually no effect because of the delays of price feeding through. As time goes on, the series of similar production-cuts made when producer stocks are steadily falling produces a greater response in price and this, together with the lags in demand, starts to manifest itself in a fall in demand. By the end of the period, the gap in production below the base case is matched by the gap of consumption below the base case, but at a very much lower level of producer stocks and a slightly lower level of consumer stocks. Eventually, the simulation indicates that the world price would increase to well over 150 cents a lb. The much more ambitious 10 per cent production-cut has qualitatively similar results, but with a very sharp price rise towards the end of the period as stocks are run down to very low levels.

The movement in export earnings mirrors that of the world price, since the fall in export quantity associated with the assumed production cut-backs is relatively marginal. The rise in export earnings over the base case figures is relatively quite small for the first few years of the simulation period, but after 1986 export earnings would have risen substantially faster than in the base case. By 1990, earnings would have risen to some 70 per cent above the base case value for the smaller production cut-back scheme, and to 200 per cent above for the larger production cut-back (see Figure 5.2).

In view of the time-path of prices and export earnings, it would clearly be important that a production cut-back scheme be given a chance to work and not be judged on its early results. The model constructed emphasizes the key role of stocks in being able to release coffee to offset the initial production cut-backs and hence to dampen the price rise. Only as stock levels are steadily depleted will the full benefits of the scheme be felt by producers. It is important not to

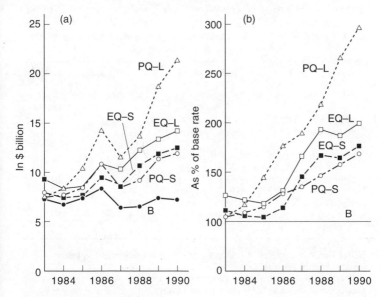

Fig. 5.2 Coffee: impact of alternative supply management schemes on export revenues, 1983–90.

Notes: PQ–S and PQ–L=production quota, smaller and larger cut-back respectively; EQ–S and EQ–L=export quota, smaller and larger cut-back respectively; B=base case. Data refer to exports from ICO-member producing countries to ICO-member consuming countries. *Source*: Appendix Table B.2.

extrapolate too positively from the results. The simulation model has allowed no production response to the higher prices (which is credible in the short run), and also has assumed full co-operation between producers. Finally, it is likely that the market would become accustomed to the lower stock/production ratio, and would not continue to force up prices as predicted by the simulation.

For the simulation period as a whole, both of the assumed production cut-backs are associated with large reductions in coffee stocks—by some 16 per cent, on average, for the smaller production cut, and by nearly 30 per cent for the larger. Coffee prices and export revenue would consequently have been higher, on average, by over 30 per cent and some 90–100 per cent, respectively (see Table 5.6).

Table 5.6 *Summary of simulation results for alternative coffee schemes: annual averages for 1983–1990 (base case quantities in million bags of 60 kg., price in US cents per lb., export earnings in $ bn., simulation results in percentage change from base case.)*

	Base case	Production cut		Export quota	
		5% p.a.	10% p.a.	130 cents/lb.	150 cents/lb.
Production	91.5	−3.4	−6.8	0	0
Consumption	78.2	−1.1	−2.9	−1.2	−1.0
Exports	61.0	−1.7	−4.2	−1.8	−2.8
Stocks:					
Producers	51.2	−20.6	−38.5	+6.3	+11.1
Consumers	20.0	−2.7	−5.8	−2.9	−4.4
Total stocks	71.1	−15.5	−29.3	+3.8	+6.8
Coffee price	115	+34	+96	+37	+58
Coffee export earnings	9.31	+31	+88	+34	+53

Notes: This table relates to producer countries members of the International Coffee Organization (ICO).

The simulated declines in exports are less than the specified cuts in production, since the latter is assumed to apply only to the eight principal producing countries.

See Table 5.5 for assumptions made for each simulation.

The export figures exclude exports to non-member countries of the ICO.

In assessing these results, it is important to note that the simulations assume that the cut-backs really are effective and that there is no leakage into the non-ICO member market, since this would have greatly dampened the price increase. The model also assumes that coffee production and consumption in non-ICO members, as well as the trade between member and non-member countries, would have been unaffected by the working of production cut-backs.

An export quota scheme

The second supply management option considered is the use of export quotas to achieve a target real coffee price. Given a target price, the coffee model can be solved for other variables. The export variable is taken as exports from ICO member producers to member consumers. With higher world prices resulting from a quota, and producer prices linked to the world price, producers' revenue rises and there is an adjustment in producer stocks.

As with the production cut-back scheme, world consumption is reduced by ever-increasing amounts, but the gap between the impacts of the 130 cents and 150 cents target real prices is almost constant. Consumer stocks are run down, especially after 1987, when the target price is much above the actual price (a very similar picture holds for producer stocks under the production cut-back option). The difference between the two policies (i.e. production cut-back and export quota) over time reflects the fact that the production cut-back is a substantial restriction on the system, while the price targets for the export quota in the early years are very near the actual and base case prices, and hence begin to have substantial impacts only in the latter half of the period.

The simulation again stresses the importance of stocks in the world coffee economy. As quotas bite to bid up prices, both consumer and producer stocks are run down which, in effect, requires a bigger cut in exports in order to force consumption down so that the market-clearing price can rise to the target.

For the simulation period as a whole, the export quota would involve a reduction in exports, compared with the base case, of almost 2 per cent a year, on average, for the smaller export cut-back (the 130 cents per lb. real price target), or almost 3 per cent a year, for the larger cut-back (150 cents real price). The consequent impact on export earnings is simulated as an increase of over 30 per cent over the base case level, on the smaller export cut-back, and over 50 per cent on the larger cut-back (see Table 5.6).

The simulations indicate that the use of export quotas to achieve a given price target for coffee produces relatively smaller gains in export revenue in the earlier years of the simulation period than in the later. For the smaller export cut (130 cents per lb. target), the export revenue of all coffee-exporting countries, including non-ICO members, would rise (in terms of US dollars) from about 7 per cent above the base case average for the years 1983–5 to 41 per cent above in 1986–8, and further to 69 per cent. above in 1989–90. The corresponding increases for the larger export cut (150 cents per lb. target) are 22, 61, and 93 per cent. respectively (Appendix Table B.2).

Country export earnings

It would have been of interest to assess the impact of the alternative supply management schemes on the export revenue in foreign currency on a country-by-country basis, as was done for cocoa. However, for coffee there is substantial local consumption and stockbuilding, unlike the case of cocoa, so that further sub-models clearing the market for each country would be required in order to distinguish exports from production. Since this would have been beyond the scope of the present study, it is not possible to give an analysis of the impact of alternative policies on export earnings at a country level. The model does, however, allow simulations to be made for the revenue of coffee producers in local currency.

Table 5.7 shows the percentage changes in producers' revenue for seven of the eight producers assumed to have participated in production or export cut-backs[3] The calculation relates predicted revenue in the 'policy on' case to that in the base case. Any changes between the two thus allow for the reduction in production or exports and the impact on producers in local currency as the rise in the world price

Table 5.7 *Simulated producer revenues of major coffee producing countries for alternative supply management schemes: annual averages for 1983–1990 (percentage change from base case)*

	Production cut		Export quota	
	Smaller cut	Larger cut	Smaller cut	Larger cut
Brazil	21	58	31	47
Colombia	14	36	22	33
Guatemala	11	28	18	28
Mexico	8	21	15	23
Côte d'Ivoire	7	18	14	21
India	14	36	22	33
Indonesia	25	71	35	55

[3] In the case of Uganda, producer prices could not be modelled, so that no local currency valuation can be made.

works back into the domestic market. It is assumed that such revenue shifts would neither affect the exchange rate nor change the relation between the world market price and the producer price. Although each country is assumed to cut production or exports by the same percentages, and faces the same world price, differences in local revenues arise because of differences in the extent and speed with which changes in the world price are passed through to local producer prices, as well as differences in supply elasticities. Brazil and Indonesia, in particular, would tend to reap differential gains because of their strong links between producer prices in local currency and the world price in US dollars, after allowing for changes in the relevant exchange rates. However, even Mexico and Côte d'Ivoire, for both of which the link between producer prices and the world price was relatively much weaker, would also have benefited significantly in terms of higher export earnings.

It will be noted that the simulations implicitly assume that coffee is a homogenous commodity. This was a necessary assumption since relevant time-series for different varieties, such as arabica and robusta, are not available. This introduces some inevitable margin of error into the country simulations to the extent that the patterns of world demand, and of world trade, move in favour of arabica varieties, while particular countries may, for example, specialize in robustas. However, any bias from this factor is not likely to change the general picture of revenue benefits accruing to all producing countries from the supply management schemes considered.

5.3   TEA

For the simulation period for tea, which is taken as from 1986 to 1990, inclusive, the fit of the dynamic solution of the tea model is reasonably good. However, the model did not explain very well the level of tea prices or tea export earnings in the year 1990 (for further discussion, see Chapter 9). A major difficulty in constructing the model was the lack of the relevant statistical series for many countries. This was particularly the case for retail tea prices (apart from the UK,

USA, and India), for prices received by tea producers, and for tea stocks in consuming countries (apart from the UK). Various proxies for missing series have been used, but there inevitably remains a margin of error in the model results.

Two possible approaches to a supply management scheme for tea are examined. The first is the use of export quotas, an approach which has already been used by producing countries in the informal arrangements for 1970 and 1971 mentioned earlier. For this reason, it may prove more acceptable as a basis for negotiating a new supply management scheme than other, untried, approaches. The second approach considered is the use of a uniform *ad valorem* tax on tea exports from all, or all the main, producing countries. Several of these have had small taxes or cesses on tea exports for government revenue purposes, at least until recent years, so that this would be a familiar mechanism, even if used for a somewhat different purpose.

An export quota scheme

Two alternative price targets have been used for the supply management simulations. The first price target is a relatively modest one, viz. that the average real tea price in the period 1986 to 1990 is raised to midway between the corresponding 1980 price and the 1986–90 average. The second price target is more ambitious, as it assumes that the average price during 1986–90 is maintained in real terms at the 1980 level. The first price target thus implies a smaller cut-back in the volume of tea supplies (compared with the 'no supply management' base case) than does the more ambitious second target (see Table 5.8).

To allow for the rise in manufactures' prices from 1986 to 1990, as measured by the UN index of unit values of manufactures exported by developed countries, the smaller export cut-back option implies a rise in the nominal tea price from $2,285 per tonne in 1986 to $2,995 in 1990. For the larger export cut-back, the corresponding nominal prices are $2,665 for 1986 rising to $3,493 in 1990. These—and corresponding prices for intermediate years—then become the exogenous values on the basis of which the model solves for the world

Table 5.8 *Assumptions made for alternative supply management schemes for tea*

	Assumption
1. Export quota	(a) *Smaller cutback*: to maintain the world price in real terms midway between 1980 and the 1986–90 average (b) *Larger cut-back*: to maintain the world price in real terms at the 1980 level
2. Uniform *ad valorem* export tax	Tax rate rising from 20% in 1986 to 40% in 1990, with mean rate over the period of 30%

export volume that would yield the targeted price paths when tea supply and demand are equated. The model also solves for the export quantity that would be forthcoming at these prices in the absence of market intervention (the base case). The difference between the two is the cut in export quantity required by this supply management policy.

As Figure 5.3 indicates, the model results show that either of the export quota cut-backs would have resulted in a

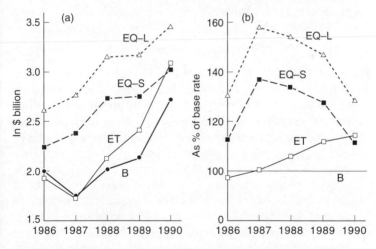

Fig. 5.3 Tea: impact of alternative supply management schemes on export revenues, 1986–90

Note: EQ–S and EQ–L=export quota, smaller and larger cut-back respectively; ET=export tax; B=base case.
Source: Appendix Table B.3

Table 5.9 *Summary of simulation results for alternative tea schemes: annual averages for 1986–1990 (base case quantity in '000 tonnes, price in $ per kg., earnings in $ bn., simulation results in percentage change from base case.)*

	Export quantity	Average tea price	Export earnings
Base case (no supply management)	995	2.13	2.12
Supply management 1. Export quota			
(a) Smaller cut	−1.0	+25	+24
(b) Larger cut	−2.0	+46	+43
2. Uniform *ad valorem* export tax	−3.9	+12	+7

Note: See Table 5.8 for assumptions made for each simulation.

substantial expansion in tea export revenue, over the simulation period; over the whole simulation period, the average annual revenue increase over the base case would have been almost 25 per cent for the smaller cut-back and over 40 per cent for the larger (Table 5.9).

A uniform ad valorem export tax

For this policy, it has been assumed that an export tax is imposed uniformly over the simulation period by four major tea-producing countries for which production and consumption equations can be estimated. These countries—India, China, Kenya, and Turkey—accounted for some 60 per cent of world tea production in 1986, and for slightly more in 1990.

For illustrative purposes, it is assumed that the tax rate is increased progressively over the simulation period, rising from 20 per cent *ad valorem* in 1986 by 5 percentage points a year until 1990 when the tax reaches 40 per cent, the average tax rate over the period thus being 30 per cent. With this assumed tax, the domestic producer and consumer prices in the four major tea-producing countries would be reduced relative to the world price by a factor proportional to the tax. This, in turn, would reduce production and increase domestic consumption, relative to the base case, and thus lead to a run-down in producer stocks and a fall in export volume.

However, there is clearly some time-lag before the tax regime works through to influence the world price. In the early years of the simulation period, the price remains close to that in the base case (see Figure 5.3), but as the assumed increase in tax rates, and the loss of earnings, begin to affect production and consumption, exports begin to fall and the world price rises towards the end of the period. By 1990, the world price (corresponding to a 40 per cent tax rate) is simulated at $3,240 per tonne, or exactly midway between the corresponding simulations for that year for the alternative export quota schemes ($3,000 per tonne for the smaller export quota cut-back and $3,490 for the larger).

The time-lag before the export tax begins to have significant effects on prices and earnings is one reason why, for the simulation period as a whole, the world tea price is estimated at only 12 per cent above the base case, even though export quantity is cut by an average of about 4 per cent a year, or double the rate of export quantity cut-back for the more ambitious export quota scheme (Table 5.9). Had the relationship between the tax rate and the associated percentage increase in export revenue held good for other rates of tax than that assumed here, then to achieve, say, a 25 per cent increase in export revenue above the base case would have required a tax rate of 106 per cent, while for an export revenue increase of 40 per cent, the tax rate would need to be raised to some 170 per cent.

Country export earnings

Simulations of the tea export earnings of individual producing countries have also been made. For the two illustrative export quota schemes, it has been assumed that the required cut in exports is shared among the five major exporting countries—India, China, Indonesia, Kenya, and Sri Lanka—in the same proportion as their shares in their combined tea exports as indicated by the base case solution. For example, if India's exports in the base case represent, say, 20 per cent of the total tea exports of the five countries, then Indian exports under the quota regime are taken to equal 20 per cent of the restricted export total required to achieve the target price.

For the export tax option, the calculations have had to exclude Sri Lanka—for lack of production and demand equations—and include Turkey. However, the movement in tea export revenue for Sri Lanka has been derived on the assumption that that country does not impose an export tax, but does benefit from the rise in the world price induced by the tax.

The simulation results for the individual producing countries are summarized in Table 5.10. Under the smaller export quota cut-back, tea export revenues would have been, on average, about 20 per cent above the base case for Sri Lanka and China, and about 25 per cent above for India, Kenya, and Indonesia. The corresponding gains on the larger cut-back would have been about 30 per cent for Sri Lanka and about 45 per cent for the other producers. For the export tax case, by contrast, there would have been marginal gains in all cases, except for India, where there would have been a marginal loss.

This outcome for India reflects the fact that India has a very large domestic market for tea and, because of the export tax there would be an incentive for traders to divert tea to the domestic market. The simulation results for India indicate that there would indeed have been such a diversion; between 1986 and 1990, domestic tea consumption is simulated to rise

Table 5.10 *Change in tea export earnings from alternative supply management schemes: annual averages for 1986–1990 (base case in $ m., simulation results in percentage increase from base case)*

	Base case	Export quota cut-back		Uniform export tax
		Smaller	Larger	
Sri Lanka	447	18	32	12
India	389	25	46	−2
China	348	21	39	9
Kenya	316	26	46	8
Indonesia	208	25	43	8

Note: See Table 5.8 for assumptions made for each simulation.

by some 90,000 tonnes (21 per cent) under the assumed export tax regime, of which one-half would come from increased Indian production, the other one-half from a fall of 25 per cent in export shipments. By contrast, tea exports from other countries would have expanded by some 30,000 tonnes (3–4 per cent) during this period, as a result of higher simulated world tea prices in the later 1980s. It would appear, therefore, that a uniform export tax regime would work to India's disadvantage in terms both of share of the world market and of the level of export earnings from tea.

6
Summary of Findings and Policy Implications

6.1 THE MAIN FINDINGS

The foreign exchange losses incurred by developing countries since the early 1980s as a result of deterioration in the terms of trade of their exports of tropical beverages have been huge, by any criterion. Over the period from 1980 to 1993, the cumulated loss totalled over \$105 bn., or more than six times the total value of their tropical beverage shipments in 1980.[1] The corresponding loss was relatively greatest for the African region, was substantial also for Latin America, but much less so for Asian countries which have a higher dependence on tea, for which real prices declined by a much smaller extent than did those for cocoa and coffee.

The terms of trade of tropical beverages deteriorated very much faster after 1985 than they had done in the first half of the 1980s. Whereas the annual terms of trade loss had averaged \$3.6 bn. a year from 1981 to 1985, the annual loss rose to \$5.6 bn. during 1986–8, and further to \$13.7 bn. in 1989–91 and \$15.9 bn. in 1992–3. The sharp rise in the rate of loss in 1989–91 largely reflected the collapse of the international cocoa and coffee agreements in 1988 and 1989 respectively. More fundamentally, the markets for both cocoa and coffee had developed a severe disequilibrium in the later 1980s as world production exceeded world demand in successive years, resulting in the accumulation of abnormally high levels of unsold stocks. For cocoa, the world surplus turned into a deficit in the early 1990s, though the stock overhang remained relatively high, while for coffee a decline in production

[1] Based on cumulated figures for terms of trade losses in Tables 2.3, 2.5, and 2.9

together with a rise in consumption led to a sharp fall in the stocks/consumption ratio after 1992. For tea, the period was also characterized by successive years of overproduction, mainly as a result of sharp expansion in output in the newer producing countries—especially Kenya and Indonesia—combined with falling demand in Britain, Canada, and South Africa.

The collapse of both the cocoa and coffee agreements signalled the failure of the international community to deal effectively with the growing crisis in the world markets for these two commodities. This failure reflects essentially a basic divergence of objectives between the developing producer countries and the developed consumer countries as regards the functioning of an international commodity agreement. As mentioned in Chapter 2, for the producers the objective in a period of oversupply and declining prices should be to regulate supplies coming on the world market so as to defend the minimum, or 'floor', price of the agreement. For the consumers, by contrast, the objective in a period of oversupply should rather be to adjust the agreed price range downward so as to keep it in line with the market trend.

In view of the objection by major consumer countries to intervention in international commodity markets in order to raise prices, even from persistently depressed levels, the question examined in the present study is whether the producer countries themselves can devise viable schemes to 'manage' supplies so as to raise depressed price levels, while reducing the stock 'overhang' to more normal levels. Some alternative supply management mechanisms on which such schemes could be based have been explored, and their probable effects on the export revenues of producing countries have been quantitatively assessed on the basis of econometric modelling and simulations.

The Supply Management Simulations

The alternative supply management schemes for which simulations were done using the new econometric models are essentially illustrative. One option studied was the use of export quotas to achieve selected levels of real prices, the selected levels being relatively modest targets so that they could be accepted as fair and reasonable by consuming countries. A second option considered was the imposition by producing countries of a uniform *ad valorem* tax, though it was found that this would not be a viable option for coffee, and was also questionable in the case of tea. In addition, for cocoa, another alternative taken was a scheme for regular reduction of the large overhang of stocks (on the lines of a similar scheme which has been operating for tin), while for both cocoa and coffee alternative percentage cuts in production were also simulated.

As was to be expected in view of the low demand elasticities for tropical beverages, prices are very sensitive to relatively small degrees of restriction of production, and/or of exports, and thus of supplies coming on the world market. Since in all the alternative cases studied the price-elasticity of demand is low, the decline in demand—as measured by the change in consumption—is generally smaller than the assumed policy cut in production or exports, thus tending to reduce stocks and raise prices. For all the alternative supply management measures, apart from the export tax, prices and export earnings would have been very substantially higher than in the 'no policy' base case. For both cocoa and tea, however, the impact of a uniform export tax on prices and export earnings is shown to be relatively quite small.

It is also of relevance, in assessing the merits of the alternative supply management schemes, to compare their effects on export earnings with the terms of trade losses actually suffered by producing countries over the simulation period. The simulation results show that production or export cutbacks of the order assumed in some of the simulations would have prevented any terms of trade losses from having incurred. Indeed, the assumed larger export or production cuts for coffee, and either of the export quota cut-backs for tea, would have resulted in sizeable net export earnings gains, after deducting the corresponding terms of trade losses. However, the assumed levels of export tax would have offset only one-sixth of the terms of trade loss for cocoa, and two-fifths of that for tea (see Table 6.1).

Table 6.1 *Gains to the export earnings of producing countries from alternative supply management schemes in relation to terms of trade losses (gains in $ bn., proportion of terms of trade loss in percentage)*

	Supply management gain			As proportion of terms of trade loss		
	Cocoa	Coffee	Tea	Cocoa	Coffee	Tea
1. Stock reduction	2.57	—	—	126	—	—
2. Export quota:						
(a) Smaller cut	—	3.17	0.51	—	76	136
(b) Larger cut	—	4.94	0.91	—	119	244
3. Production cut:						
(a) Smaller cut	0.78	2.91	—	38	70	—
(b) Larger cut	1.56	8.16	—	76	197	—
4. Uniform export tax	0.35	—	0.51	17	—	40

Notes: Annual average gain in export earnings over the simulation period relates to 1985–90 for cocoa; 1983–90 for coffee; 1986–90 for tea.

For definitions of assumed rate of stock depletion, smaller and larger cuts in exports and production, and of the assumed rate of export tax, see *Notes* to Tables 5.2, 5.5 and 5.8.

Operational Issues

The simulation results may also help in selecting the most efficient type of supply management for a particular market. For this purpose the 'operational efficiency' of a supply management scheme can be defined as the percentage increase in price or export earnings which results from a given percentage cut in production, exports, or stocks, or from a given *ad valorem* export tax. On this definition, an export tax would seem to be the least efficient approach for the tropical beverage crops. Thus, for cocoa, the percentage increase in export earnings resulting from a uniform export tax would be only 40 per cent of the tax rate (see Table 6.2), so that if earnings were to be increased by, say, 50 per cent, the tax would need to be set at 125 per cent. Equally, for tea, the tax rate would have to be over 200 per cent for export earnings to rise by 50 per cent. By contrast, the price and earnings elasticities for export quota schemes are all relatively high. Thus, for both

Table 6.2 *Elasticities of price and export earnings with respect to changes in instrumental variables*

	Cocoa		Coffee		Tea	
	Price	Earnings	Price	Earnings	Price	Earnings
1. Stock reduction	2.2	1.8	—	—	—	—
2. Export quota:						
(a) Smaller cut	5.8	4.4	20.5	19.0	25.4	24.1
(b) Larger cut	3.9	2.9	20.3	18.9	23.0	21.6
3. Production cut:						
(a) Smaller cut	—	—	10.0	9.1	—	—
(b) Larger cut	—	—	14.1	12.9	—	—
4. Uniform export tax	0.53	0.40	—	—	0.39	0.24

Source: Table 6.1

coffee and tea a 50 per cent rise in export earnings above the base case would have required an export quota cut of some 2–4 per cent of the base case export quantity, in each case. For cocoa, however, the export cut would have had to be more severe—between 11 and 17 per cent of the base case quantity—to achieve a 50 per cent rise in export earnings.

A stock reduction scheme, such as the one used as an illustrative example for cocoa, would also be 'efficient' in the sense used here. If this example is taken as representative of the impact of a cocoa stock reduction scheme of different magnitudes, then a 50 per cent increase in cocoa export earnings would result from an average reduction of 28 per cent in the level of stocks. However, as can be seen from Table 6.2, the stock reduction approach would not appear to be as efficient as an export quota scheme, on the criterion used here.

In addition to operational efficiency, producing countries which were considering the adoption of a supply management scheme would also need to consider the other operational issues listed in Chapter 1, namely the probable ease or difficulty of negotiation, probable consumer reactions, the ease or difficulty of policing the scheme, and the assurance of support by the main producing countries.

As regards negotiation, it would seem likely that agreement on a uniform *ad valorem* export tax could be reached more readily than agreement on export quotas, since the latter inevitably involves disputes regarding market shares, whereas a uniform tax could be imposed without interference with the relative competitiveness of different producing countries. However, producing countries may well prefer not to choose the tax option in view of the high rate of tax that would be required to achieve a substantial gain in export revenue so as to offset at least some significant proportion of the term of trade loss. A stock reduction scheme (for cocoa), whether or not supported by export quotas—informal quotas if the scheme is modelled on the existing tin scheme— would also involve relative share negotiations.

It would also be important for the success of a producer-only supply management scheme that the price objective should be a relatively modest one, so as to avoid consumer hostility including possible measures to undermine the scheme. The illustrative simulations in the present study were chosen to conform to this criterion. For example, for cocoa, the rise in simulated export earnings above the base case represented, for all the alternative schemes, only one-half or less of the foreign exchange loss associated with the terms of trade deterioration over the simulation period. For coffee, the proportion of the terms of trade loss offset by a 5 per cent cut in production, or an export quota that maintained the indicator price at the mid- point of the range of the 1983 agreement, was in the region of 70–5 per cent. On this criterion, the larger production or export cuts simulated for coffee, which would have yielded gains exceeding the terms of trade loss, might be judged as excessive. An additional safeguard for the consuming countries would arise if—as suggested at the beginning of Chapter 4—a supply management scheme were operated within the framework of an international commodity agreement involving consumers as well as producers, on the lines of the production regulation scheme incorporated in the new international cocoa agreement.

Reliable policing of a supply management scheme operated by producer countries only would generally be more difficult than if consumer countries also participated in the arrangement. None the less, a producer-only scheme based on export quotas should function reliably, since an automatic check is provided by official statistics of actual exports, and penalties can be imposed for over-shipments. Alternative schemes based on stock reduction or cuts in production would be more difficult to police in view of the inadequacy of stock and output statistics in a number of producing countries, while an export tax scheme could be evaded, to a greater or lesser extent, by changes in domestic tax and subsidy arrangements. An accepted need for rigorous and objective policing would clearly give preference, in this respect, to an export quota over other alternative schemes.

6.2   POLICY IMPLICATIONS

An important conclusion of the present study is that for the tropical beverage crops the regulation of supplies coming to the world market with the aim of raising persistently depressed levels of prices and export earnings would be a technically feasible operation. Indeed, if the supply management involved, in addition, a significant reduction in the short-term price and earnings instability of the tropical beverage markets, this would be an added bonus for both producers and consumers.

The various model simulations, which broadly covered the second half of the 1980s, have shown that over this period the sharp deterioration in tropical beverage prices, and the consequent foreign exchange losses for producing countries—both of which reflected a growing surplus of world production above the level of world consumption—would have been wholly or largely avoided or, at least, substantially alleviated, had some effective supply management been in operation. The implication of this finding is that for the 1990s also, a supply management approach with similar objectives would be appropriate, so long as market forces by themselves fail to eliminate persistent excess supply. This conclusion is consistent with the decisions made in recent years by both the cocoa- and coffee-producing countries to introduce supply management schemes, as discussed in Chapter 3.

Indeed, the decade ahead seems likely to be dominated by relatively slow growth in the developed countries, which are the major markets for both cocoa and coffee, while production of all three beverage crops would appear likely to expand, partly as a result of continuing pressure to increase exports to help meet debt service obligations, as well as the likelihood of greater competition among producing countries in the absence of supply management. Against this background, market forces alone cannot be expected to bring any significant alleviation of the foreign exchange difficulties of many producing countries over the medium term.

This rather gloomy prognosis is supported by World Bank price projections up to the year 2005,which indicate that the coffee price boom of 1994 and 1995 will prove to be a temporary phenomenon, and that by the year 2005 real coffee prices are unlikely to be substantially different from their 1990 levels. Cocoa prices in 2005 are projected to be nearly 10 per cent above 1990 in real terms, while for tea the corresponding projection shows a decline of almost 30 per cent (World Bank, 1995).

Finally, it is important to emphasize two important caveats to the above policy implications of the simulations results. First, all the simulations have been based on the assumption that the selected supply management schemes would be fully supported by all the principal producing countries including, if possible, countries which, though not now large producers, have the potential for substantial output expansion in the future. If this assumption does not hold, a supply management scheme is unlikely to be viable. Clearly, if one low-cost producer has plans to expand production so as to capture a larger share of the export market, its refusal to support a supply management scheme could effectively undermine it. In such a case, which may well apply to cocoa, the low-cost producer has the choice of exporting a higher volume at a relatively low price, or a somewhat lower volume at a substantially higher price. Since world demand for the tropical beverage crops is relatively inelastic, the latter choice would produce the higher export revenue.

The second important caveat is that supply management cannot by itself provide a panacea for the long-term problems of commodities in persistent oversupply. For many producing countries, especially those heavily dependent on cocoa or coffee with falling market shares, it is essential to develop viable programmes of diversification into other activities, including not only the production and export of other primary commodities for which world demand is expanding (i.e. 'horizontal' diversification), but also 'vertical' diversification into processing, manufacturing, or service industries. To the extent that supply management can increase export earnings from depressed levels, some proportion of the increased earnings should be made available to help finance needed diversification and structural change. In this way, supply management could make a significant contribution to laying the basis for sustained growth in the future, as well as alleviating the immediate and short-term foreign exchange difficulties of countries heavily dependent on the production and export of tropical beverage crops.

II

Econometric Analysis

7

The World Cocoa Market

7.1 THE DEMAND FOR COCOA

The demand for cocoa is derived from the demands for the final products in which it is used. The predominant use of cocoa is in the production of chocolate, which is used in a wide range of products, usually being combined with other inputs as in chocolate biscuits. The share by weight of cocoa in these final products is usually less than 50 per cent in aggregate, so that there is no simple correspondence between the final demand for chocolate products and the demand for cocoa.

Most statistical studies have worked with a reduced-form demand equation in which the demand for cocoa is related to factors which directly impinge on the demand for chocolate, such as income. Only if there were a constant relation between the volumes of chocolate and cocoa and between the prices of chocolate and cocoa can such an approach be fully justified.

Evidence from many countries suggests that over time both the volume and price links have changed. This can be due to changes in the relative prices of the inputs which are combined to make the final products and also to changes in consumer preferences for the different types of products which use chocolate in their manufacture.

A full econometric study would need to identify both the final demand for chocolate, the use of cocoa in chocolate manufacture, and the link from the cocoa price to the price of chocolate products, in order to understand the links between changes in the price of cocoa and the resulting impact on the demand for cocoa. A comparison of such a structural approach with the reduced-form approach is discussed in some detail in the Annexe to this chapter in relation to modelling the demand for cocoa in the UK. For the main model, however, limited data availability constrains the analysis to the use of the reduced-form approach.

Modelling issues

All single commodity demand functions need to allow for changes in income, population, the price of the product, the price of close substitutes, and the dynamics of adjustment. Each of these is discussed in turn.

(i) *Income.* Since chocolate (cocoa) is consumed by householders the best measure of income would be total personal income in real terms. Where this is not available real Gross National Product (GNP) can be used. The impact of income on demand is expected to be positive since chocolate is known from previous studies not to be an inferior good.

(ii) *Population.* If all members of the population have similar demands for chocolate then growth in population should produce a proportionate effect on its consumption. Per capita demand should be a function of per capita real income, prices, etc., so that total demand is the per capita demand function multiplied by the population. Experiments for the UK showed no significant effects for the age structure (proportion of children, etc.), possibly because this changes only rather slowly.

(iii) *Own-prices.* The own-price of chocolate (cocoa) should also be expressed in real terms (relative to the retail price index) to capture the general substitution against all other goods. The effect is expected to be negative. The price effect would be expected to be greater when the demand for chocolate is measured than when the demand for cocoa is measured, because in the latter case the impact of a 1 per cent rise in cocoa prices is less than a 1 per cent rise in chocolate prices (because of the existence of other inputs) which leads to the change in the demand for cocoa itself.

(iv) *Cross-prices.* When the final demand for chocolate is analysed, the relevant prices are of similar consumer goods, e.g. sugar confectionery or plain biscuits. Here the effect is expected to be positive for the relative price of substitutes to chocolate. If the demand for cocoa is analysed, the picture is more complex, since as well as substitute goods in final consumption there are the prices of other factors of production to consider. For example, sugar is also used in the manufacture of chocolate products. Depending on whether this is a complementary or substitute factor of production, a rise in the price of sugar could lead to an increase in the demand for cocoa (through input substitution) or a decrease (through the general effects of a rise in price of the end-product).

(v) *Dynamics of demand.* In the demand for chocolate consumers may not immediately respond fully to changes in chocolate prices or in income. Only with time will consumption habits adjust to altered circumstances. This effect may be combined with a change in tastes where a steady shift in preferences can sometimes be picked up by a lagged dependent variable. For the demand for cocoa there may be additional lags as firms take time to decide to vary the proportion of cocoa used to make chocolate products.

A separate issue for econometric modelling is the functional form to be used. Two specifications have been widely used. The simplest case, especially when demand is part of a large simultaneous system, is the linear function, e.g.

$$c = \alpha + \beta P + \delta y, \tag{1}$$

where c is per capita consumption; y is per capita real income; and P is the real chocolate price.

As is well known, such a function does not exhibit constant price or income elasticities.

$$e_P = \beta P/(\alpha + \beta P + \delta y) \tag{2}$$

The elasticity varies (between zero and infinity) depending on the price and income levels at which it is evaluated. It is conventional to evaluate both price and income elasticities at the means of the data sample. At the means of the independent variables the least squares line passes through the mean of the dependent variable so that the (per capita) demand elasticity can be written:

$$e_P = \beta \bar{P}/\bar{c} \tag{2a}$$

At all other levels the value of the dependent variable has to be calculated from the fitted value of the regression equation as in (2) rather than by using the actual value which will include a non-zero residual. For linear models different studies cannot simply be compared through their published elasticities since these will depend on their sample means.

An alternative approach is to use a double-log model which constrains the responses to constant elasticities at all data points:

$$\log c = \alpha' + \beta' \log P + \delta' \log y, \tag{3}$$

where β' and δ' are the elasticities. There is no a priori reason to believe that either will automatically fit the data better, so the choice will be made on goodness of fit of the actual values and on computational simplicity considerations.

Previous results

There have been a number of studies estimating the demand for cocoa. Some of the major studies are briefly reviewed below.

(i) *Behrman (1965)*. The dependent variable in this study is based on an estimate of final cocoa consumption per capita. This is related to per capita real disposable income, the real price of cocoa, and the real price of sugar. The cocoa price in the various countries used is calculated in two ways: either as the average import unit value of cocoa, or the New York spot price times the appropriate exchange rate. Both prices are deflated by the wholesale price index for raw materials. The sample period is 1950–61 and a linear demand function is used. Estimation is by ordinary least squares (OLS) and by instrumental variables (in case of simultaneity bias). The results show income elasticities ranging from −1.58 for the USA to 0.81 for Germany; own-price elasticities ranging from −0.14 for France to 0.02 for Germany, and cross-price elasticities from 0.66 for the UK to −0.84 for France.

(ii) *Behrman (1968)*. In this study Behrman adopts a similar per capita linear model. Short lags (half a year) are introduced on the real cocoa and sugar prices, and the real price of soya (a substitute input) is added. The data period is 1948 to 1964 and more countries are added to the sample. The longer period shows higher income elasticities and higher own price elasticities than those for the earlier study. Soya appears to be a strong substitute in production.

(iii) *Akiyama and Duncan (1984)*. This study relates the per capita final consumption of cocoa to per capita real GDP and to current and lagged real cocoa prices (based on import unit values) using a double log formulation. The data period is from 1961 to 1978, the country groupings being much broader than in Behrman's studies. These authors also fit a total world demand function to world GDP and current and lagged deflated cocoa prices. The income elasticity is 0.55 and the long-term price elasticity is -0.24. They point out that these aggregate results are similar to ones obtained earlier by Behrman and others. They also refer to a study by the International Cocoa Organization published in 1975 which gave rather similar results for the industrialized countries. An important feature of the Akiyama and Duncan study is the complete coverage of world demand and the treatment of the planned economies as responding to domestic income and prices in a similar fashion to market economies.

(iv) *Groenendaal and Vingerhoets (1988)*. This study uses data from 1955 to 1982 in a double log model. Consumption of cocoa per capita is related to real GNP per capita, the real import price of cocoa and the real price of sugar. A lagged dependent variable is added to provide dynamic adjustment. Equations for four country groupings are estimated within a simultaneous system. Long-run income elasticity estimates range from 0.25 for North America to 0.66 for Eastern Europe and (former) Soviet Union, while long-run price elasticities vary from -0.15 for Western Europe to -0.40 for the world excluding North America, Western and Eastern Europe. The short-run elasticities (of price and income) are about 75 per cent of the long-run elasticities, suggesting that demand does not adjust fully within one period.

(v) *UNCTAD/ICCO (1991)*. This study uses a double log specification in which the per capita consumption of cocoa is related to per capita real income and the real price of cocoa, while the lagged dependent variable is also included. The cocoa price is the world cocoa price converted by the exchange rate. The data are from 1961 to 1988 (for most countries).

Certain features of the results stand out. Price elasticities are usually low—in a range around −0.2. Income elasticities are often higher (but here there is much less agreement between the various studies). The differences in groupings of countries used is clearly important, particularly in the context of a world price-determining model where all demand must be accounted for.

Present study

The scope of the present study is similar to that of previous work, but is constrained by the requirement that demand be integrated into a world supply–demand model where price clears the market. This has two important implications. Firstly, all consumption must be accounted for, and secondly cocoa prices used must all relate to a central market price: were different prices (or unit values) to be used in different markets then there would need to be extra equations explaining the simultaneous determination of all the separate prices. In order to avoid this complexity, the simplifying assumption is made that the same price for raw cocoa, adjusted by local exchange rates, rules in every market.

In order to keep the overall model relatively simple, attention is focused on the derived demand for cocoa in each market, rather than on the final demand for products containing cocoa. Hence final consumption of cocoa is the focal variable for each country, defined as grindings in the country plus net imports of cocoa products (in bean equivalent), plus net imports of chocolate and chocolate products (both in bean equivalent). This measure is the nearest to actual final consumption of cocoa during the year but, since no data for stock changes of cocoa and chocolate products are available, there can be some year-to-year fluctuations relating to stock movements rather than to consumption itself.

The countries selected were all the major consumers for which lengthy time-series exist, i.e. the USA, Germany, Japan, France, the UK, together with some middle-sized countries (Spain, Belgium, Switzerland, and Canada). One major consumer, the Soviet Union, gave problems for modelling because of lack of income, price, and exchange rate data. Rather than attempt to fit a standard demand model to the former socialist countries of Eastern Europe, their demands are taken as exogenous. Once all these individual countries have been modelled (accounting for some 70 per cent of total world consumption in 1990), there is a small residual bloc which has to be lumped together as a 'rest of the world' sector. It is not possible to identify exactly matching macro-economic data for this bloc, so that indices for developing countries as a whole are used for GDP and for consumer prices. No reliable figure exists for the weighted average exchange rate, so that the dollar is taken as a proxy for the local currency. Although these variables are clearly measured with error, it is desirable to estimate some of the effect of changes in cocoa prices. For simulation purposes, only the price variable will be altered so that an equation picking up its effect, while other misspecified variables (such as the exchange rate) remain constant, may be adequate.

The form of the demand equations is similar to that in previous studies. Annual data for the period 1961 to 1990 are used and per capita final consumption of cocoa is related to the real price of cocoa in the local market (Ghana spot price in London times the exchange rate deflated by the consumer price index), to real GNP per capita, and to the real raw sugar price in local currency (price in London times the exchange rate deflated by the consumer price index). Lags on all variables as well as the lagged dependent variable were included, as was a time trend. Experiments with linear and double log form were carried out, but in all cases the linear model performed at least as well as the log-linear model and so it was preferred (see Section A.1.1 in the Statistical Appendix). In several cases there was evidence of a dynamic adjustment to changes in the explanatory variables. The lagged dependent variable was often significant, while in some cases current cocoa prices were insignificant while lagged prices were significant. In such cases (the UK, France, the USA), it appears that it takes at least one period for cocoa prices to affect the final demand for cocoa.

The long- and short-run (one-period impact) price and income elasticities evaluated at sample means are shown in Table 7.1.

The long-run price elasticities are fairly similar to those found in previous studies, but the addition of more recent years appears to pull most values towards the range −0.1 to −0.2. Income elasticities are also fairly similar, with the exception of that for the USA which is substantially higher than for other studies (except that of Behrman). The short-run elasticities are generally lower than the long-run values, indicating that the demand for cocoa takes time to adjust fully to changes in prices and incomes.

For Eastern Europe, the Soviet Union, and China there are no suitable data to estimate a conventional demand equation. It seems likely that for these countries, cocoa imports were related to foreign currency availability. A simple model in which total cocoa consumption of this group of countries is related to the current (and lagged) dollar price of cocoa was tried, but the results of the estimation produced such a poor fit ($R^2 = 0.21$) that it was decided to treat the sector as exogenous. This implies that its consumption is unchanged in the policy simulations over the same period.

For the rest of the world sector (total world demand less the nine countries estimated individually and less the former Soviet Union, Eastern Europe, and China), it is possible to

Table 7.1 *Estimated price and income elasticities of demand for cocoa*

	Price		Income	
	Short run	Long run	Short run	Long run
Canada	−0.22	−0.22	0.09	0.09
USA	−0.15	−0.15	1.81	1.81
Belgium	−0.10	−0.10	0.62	0.62
France	−0.09	−0.09	0.77	0.77
Germany, Fed. Rep.	−0.07	−0.14	0.11	0.24
Spain	−0.34	−0.68	1.18	1.18
Switzerland	−0.09	−0.09	0.67	0.67
UK	−0.12	−0.31	0.16	0.42
Japan	−0.09	−0.51	0.19	0.38

Source: Section A.1.1

find proxies for real GDP and consumer prices. However, there is no exchange rate or population series available for the developing world over such a long period. Accordingly, total consumption is related to real GDP in the developing world and the dollar price of cocoa deflated by an index of consumer prices in the developing world. The equation was fitted for the period 1976–89.

The complete demand block of the model is evaluated by obtaining the fitted values of the nine countries and multiplying these by the known population to obtain estimated levels of total cocoa consumption. To this is added the estimated level of developing world consumption and the actual level of consumption in the former Soviet Union, Eastern Europe, and China. This estimated world consumption of cocoa for the period 1976 to 1989 is correlated with the actual total: the squared correlation is 0.983 (with a standard error of estimate of 31 compared to a mean of 1,586,000 tonnes) indicating that the models were able to predict total consumption with a high degree of accuracy.

7.2 THE SUPPLY OF COCOA

Econometric modelling of the supply of cocoa has focused on two separate factors: first, those which affect the stock of trees and their potential yield; second, those which modify the potential yields and influence the actual output of cocoa beans. The potential output of cocoa depends on the stock of cocoa trees of various ages and the yield characteristics associated with the age of the trees. The pure age factor has been the dominant concern, although recently the introduction of high-yielding hybrid varieties has meant that yields and output have risen because of a shift in the decision as to what type of tree to plant.

The agronomic features of cocoa production have been described by several authors (e.g. Bateman 1965; Simmons and Miranowski 1980). Cocoa trees produce no yield at all up to a first threshold age, then yields jump to a first plateau level; after a few years there is a second jump in yield to a higher plateau level which is sustained for a large number of years. Most trees survive many years and only towards the end of their lifetime do the yields fall. The introduction of new varieties of hybrid stock has produced a yield curve which starts to rise earlier and at higher levels. Hence the total potential output depends crucially on the age structure of the trees. Where the stock of trees has a large component of recent planting, total output can be expected to rise for several years even though the area remains constant. Where the average age is very high, however, output can be expected to fall (although this is a more gradual process).

The first set of explanatory variables in the aggregate supply function are thus those which relate to the decisions to plant all of the bearing stock of trees and, given the fact that all trees require some time before yielding, all such variables must be operating with a lag (usually of five or more years). Analysis of the yields of cocoa trees has also shown that there are several factors which can alter the yield of a given stock of trees with a given age profile. These factors are both agronomic and economic. Some models have combined both sets of factors into a single output equation while others have separated the investment (acreage) and production (yield) factors.

Area planted and area harvested

An early statement of the interrelation between age and output is the study by Bateman (1965). The potential output at the current time (Q_t^*) depends on the acreages planted at different times in the past and yield factors associated with the varying age of the trees. The amount planted in a given year depends on the discounted stream of future of expected real cocoa prices and the discounted stream of future expected real prices for a competitor crop (coffee). Price expectations are assumed to be based on an adaptive expectations model. Hence, nominal cocoa (and coffee) prices and a general country-specific price deflator are seen as the variables affecting planting:

$$X_t = \alpha_0 + \alpha_1 P_t^* + \alpha_2 C_t^*, \tag{4}$$

where X_t is area planted; P_t^* is the discounted stream of expected future real cocoa prices; and C_t^* is the discounted stream of expected future real coffee prices.

Subsequent econometric studies such as Behrman (1968), Adams and Behrman (1976), Akiyama and Duncan (1984), and Groenendaal and Vingerhoets (1988) have all adopted a similar approach to describing the determinants of planting. With no systematic data available on direct costs such as labour, capital costs, etc., the use of a local consumer price index has generally served as a proxy for the direct costs of planting. With rather poor data available on acreage it is not possible to measure new planting directly. Not only are the reported data on the total acreage under cocoa of variable quality, there are also no data on the abandonment of acreage. Given this approach to planting it follows that the total acreage under cocoa at any time has to be modelled as the sum of all previous plantings—or the increment in acreage as a function of the factors currently affecting the decision to plant.

Studies such as Akiyama and Duncan have focused not on the total area under cocoa but on the area harvested (for which the statistics are more reliable). Because there is a lag between planting and yielding their model relates the area harvested to prices with a lag. In theory this lag should start at the age of the youngest trees able to be harvested and go back until the age of the oldest trees still in production. In practice, the real prices are lagged between three and five years, together with lagged dependent variables (which carry the effects of earlier prices) and a long lag of thirty years which allows for depreciation. The effect of the lagged dependent variables is to allow the equation to approximate one in which the change in harvested area is related to real prices lagged between three and five years. Their estimated elasticities of acreage response with respect to the producer price for the period 1965–80 range from 0.03 for Brazil, Ecuador, and Papua New Guinea to 0.09 for Côte d'Ivoire and Cameroon. For all these countries, the long-run elasticity is in the region of 0.60. These elasticities suggest that if the real price rises permanently then, over the long run, there is a substantial response in the amount of acreage planted.

A key step in relating acreage harvested to prices at the time of planting is to identify the lags before bearing. Ady (1968) assumed this to be nine years, Bateman (1965) took eight years, Behrman (1968) between six and ten years for different countries, Adams and Behrman (1976) six years, while Akiyama and Duncan (1984) take two or three years. Thus, a wide range of start-up times has been assumed, but an important factor has been the introduction of new hybrid varieties which begin to yield earlier. As these have been progressively introduced, the lag between the change in acreage harvested and past prices has shortened.

The output of cocoa

The output of cocoa has been related to three sets of factors— the acreage harvested, the average yield, and various agronomic (e.g. weather) and economic factors (e.g. the use of pesticides). There is a key interaction between area and yield due to the age structure of the trees, as pointed out above. Not only does the tree not bear any harvest for a number of years, its yield also varies greatly over its lifetime. There is a second jump in yield around the eleventh to fifteenth years, according to Behrman and Bateman, followed by a lengthy plateau of some fifteen to twenty years and then a steady decline. Hence, the average yield per acre depends on the age structure of the tree stock. Individual studies, such as that by Behrman and Bateman have introduced these long lags on prices into the output equation in an attempt to pick up the sharp changes in yields associated with these particular lags.

The introduction of hybrid varieties has not only altered the age at which trees start to yield, it has also affected the general levels of yield themselves. The greater the proportion of the tree stock that is of this type, the greater will be the average yield. Akiyama and Duncan, in their production equations, introduce a variable for the share of hybrid planting in total planting for Brazil and Côte d'Ivoire. In the absence of adequate data this yield factor could be modelled by a trend, although it would not be very satisfactory for extrapolation purposes.

There are thus two distinct approaches to modelling the effect of area on output. One, exemplified by Behrman and Bateman, substitutes out acreage completely and relates output (or changes in output) to prices lagged a large number of years. The other approach, exemplified by Akiyama and Duncan, is to relate production to current acreage harvested and a yield factor. Given that there are some acreage data available it seems sensible to follow the latter route where possible.

The second group of variables are those which transform potential output into actual output. Exogenous factors, such as rainfall and humidity (Bateman, and Akiyama and Duncan) have been used for certain countries, but such data are not generally available. Simmons and Miranowski (1980) point out that the use of pesticides and fertilizers had produced substantial impacts in some countries, but again time-series data are not generally available. All studies have also included the current or previous year's real producer price in an attempt to measure the short-run supply response of farmers with a given area of cocoa. Several studies have found only very low values for the short-run price elasticities. Behrman found significant values for Brazil (0.53) and Cameroon (0.68), while Akiyama and Duncan found values ranging between 0.1 and 0.2, with the world average at 0.14. Groenendaal and Vingerhoets found a world value of 0.23 with a substantial value only for Côte d'Ivoire (0.42).

The effect of prices on supply has been shown to depend on a short-run impact (due to intensity of harvesting, etc.) and a long-run impact through planting. Combining these two effects gives the total long-run price elasticity of supply. These are the values most easily compared, since they essentially all allow for the same factors. The results of different studies are shown in Table 7.2. These estimates show a reasonable measure of agreement except for the very low values for Ghana and Nigeria identified by Akiyama and Duncan. There is also strong evidence that the short-run elasticity of supply is substantially lower than the long-run elasticity, which gives rise to the possibility of long cycles in cocoa prices as supply responds slowly to exogenous shocks.

Table 7.2 *Estimated long-run supply elasticities for cocoa*

	Behrman (1946–64)	Akiyama and Duncan (1965–80)	Groenendaal and Vingerhoets (1955–82)
Cameroon	1.81	0.59	0.73
Côte d'Ivoire	0.80	0.59	0.82
Ghana	0.71	0.13	0.38
Nigeria	0.45	0.11	0.47
Brazil	0.95	0.54	0.29
Ecuador	0.28	0.54	
Dominican Republic	0.15	—	0.28
Venezuela	0.38	—	
Other Latin America and Caribbean	—	—	
Papua New Guinea	—	0.54	0.50
Rest of world	—	0.21	
World average	—	0.42	0.54

Notes: The elasticity for 'Rest of world' given by Akiyama and Duncan includes Latin America (except Brazil and Ecuador). The elasticity for Papua New Guinea and 'Rest of world' shown for Van Groenendaal and Vingerhoets relates to 'Asia and Oceania'.

A model of cocoa supply

The present study is constrained by the need to rely on published data, and to be in a form suitable to integrate with the demand block in order to give an integrated picture of the world cocoa market. The output figures in particular need to be consistent with the supply data, so that the implicit stock change figure is not contaminated by differences between different sources.

The countries chosen for individual study are determined by the importance of their percentage shares in total world production in 1990: Côte d'Ivoire (29.8 per cent), Brazil (14.4 per cent), Ghana (12.3 per cent), Malaysia (10.1 per cent), Nigeria (6.7 per cent), Cameroon (5.3 per cent), and Indonesia (4.8 per cent).

All other producers together accounted for 16.6 per cent. Within the period from the mid-1960s (when data start on a consistent basis) there have been some very large changes in the absolute production and relative shares of some countries. World production rose from 1.5m. tonnes in 1965 to 2.4m. tonnes in 1990. The absolute volume of production fell substantially in Ghana and Nigeria, and increased substantially in Côte d'Ivoire, Brazil, Indonesia, and Malaysia. Such large relative changes in production of a primary commodity are very unusual and are related to the decision to diversify crops in the two new producers (Indonesia and Malaysia), coupled with output losses in Ghana and in Nigeria (the area figures appear to be particularly unreliable for the latter country).

Production equations

The present study follows Akiyama and Duncan in separating the output and acreage variables into separate equations. Output is taken to be a function of the acreage *harvested*, the real producer price of cocoa, and possibly a trend variable to allow for rising yields per acre in those countries which have gradually introduced the hybrid varieties. Lags on prices have been tried in order to allow for delays in harvesting decisions in response to changes in producer prices. No specific allowance is made for the age structure of the tree stock, given the general lack of published data for lengthy periods. It is expected that a trend might pick up the effects of falling (rising) average tree age, thus raising (reducing) average productivity.

The dependent variable in the production equations is the level of production in the 'cocoa year' as reported by the ICCO. Examination of these data reveals some exceptionally large short-run changes for some countries. Although general growing conditions can severely affect yields (but not acreage in the short run), it does appear that production figures must be treated with some caution.

The main independent variable in the output equations is expected to be the acreage harvested, given the low short-run price elasticities of supply found in previous studies. Here the data are known to be unreliable, with both ICCO and FAO giving warnings on data quality, and even estimating some values themselves. There can, of course, be cycles in production as old areas are abandoned and new areas enter, and it is possible that short-run economic and climatic factors could affect farmers' decisions on how much to harvest of the bearing acreage. However, the fluctuations in reported acreage are too large and too temporary to be reconciled by such factors, so that there must be data errors. It is expected that the harvested area in the current year will be the appropriate variable, but experiments with lagged values were carried out in case recording problems meant that the previous year's value was more relevant.

The appropriate price for studying farmers' decisions and the intensity with which they harvest the crop and undertake horticultural practices which have an immediate (within the year) impact on output, is the producer price deflated by a measure of opportunity costs. The latter is taken to be the local consumer price in the absence of more detailed information on the farming sector. Producer prices themselves are determined by other factors and their link to the world market price is discussed below. Because of the possibility that past as well as present prices can affect behaviour, lagged real producer prices are tried in addition to current prices.

The output equations, which are estimated in linear form (log-linear versions showing no substantial difference in performance) also have a linear time trend added in order to capture any trends in output not related to the acreage harvested. The estimation period is generally from 1965 to 1990, but for certain countries a shorter period had to be used because of data deficiencies.

In order to close the model on the output side, an equation for 'rest of the world' production is required. The total output of the world, less that of the seven countries explicitly modelled, is related to the rest of the world acreage and the Ghana spot price in dollars deflated by the developing world cost of living index (as used for modelling 'rest of the world' demand).

The estimated output equations are given in Section A.1.2(a). Two general features stand out. The goodness of fit is often poorer than for country demand equations, even after some experimentation with varying the lags of the independent variables. The second feature is that for some countries producer prices are not significant, while for others the relationship is weak. This is very much in line with the findings of other econometric studies. For some countries it has been necessary to omit observations because data were not available for explanatory variables (e.g. Brazil for 1986 to 1990).

Although the goodness of fit as measured by the correlation coefficient is satisfactory, for certain countries the Durbin–Watson statistic is significant and suggests that there may be misspecification or serious measurement error. Since none of the variants improved the goodness of fit it was decided to leave the equations as reported.

The short-run supply elasticities of output, evaluated at the means of the data, range from zero for Côte d'Ivoire, Cameroon, Indonesia, and 'rest of the world' to 0.17 for Brazil and Nigeria, 0.44 for Ghana, and 1.05 for Malaysia. These values are not dissimilar to those from previous studies. Malaysia, which only recently has become a major producer, has a very high elasticity based on a lag of two years. This long lag (which fitted the data best) may be capturing some of the effect of rising yields not correlated with a simple time trend.

In every case the coefficient on area is highly significant and it tends to be higher in those countries which have adopted a programme of planting substantial amounts of the higher-yielding hybrid varieties.

The overall fit of the output equations is checked by taking the fitted values from all the equations, supplemented by actual values for those years where no equation was estimated, and correlating this predicted sum against actual world production for the period 1967 to 1990. This equation has an overall correlation of 85 per cent. The intercept is near zero and the slope near unity, suggesting that the prediction of aggregate output, although not as accurate as that for aggregate demand, is quite successful. Given the data limitations, it is unlikely that substantial improvements could be effected.

Acreage equations

The second part of the supply model is the block of equations explaining the area harvested in each of the main producer countries. As explained above, the area harvested at a point in time is expected to be related to cumulated decisions on planting. Given that there is a substantial lag between planting and yielding, the factors determining planting will appear in the harvesting equations with this lag.

The basic formulation suggests that, when the producer price of cocoa is high relative to opportunity costs, net planting will be high and when the price is low net planting will be low, or even negative, when abandonments are greater than planting. The total area at a point in time is thus a function of the whole history of prices. This is modelled by relating the level of the area harvested to a lagged real price and to a lagged value of the acreage harvested (the formulation used by Akiyama and Duncan). It can be seen that subtracting the level of the previous year's acreage from both sides of such an equation yields a transformed equation in which the change in acreage is related to the lagged price and to the lagged dependent variable (which will have a different coefficient). This latter formulation is that adopted by Van Groenendaal and Vingerhoets and is closely related to earlier work on supply in which the change in acreage harvested is related to lagged prices. The real price used to explain the acreage decision is the local producer price deflated by the local consumer price index, as for the output equations.

Experiments on functional form showed that in general a log-linear model was preferable for all countries, except for Brazil. Experiments on the optimum lag for the real producer price and on the number of terms in lagged acreage were also carried out. For several countries the lags on prices were long (between seven and nine years) confirming agronomic discussions on the nature of the yield pattern for cocoa trees. Only for Malaysia, where hybrid cocoa has been extensively used, and for Côte d'Ivoire, were the lags shorter.

The results, shown in detail in Section A.1.2(b), were generally good and were established for a wider range of the major producers than in earlier studies. However, the case of Nigeria serves to warn that the data on acreage are suspect. For Nigeria the reported area harvested does not change between 1978 and 1990, which makes econometric modelling pointless. All the results must be treated with a degree of caution, given the recognized difficulties of obtaining accurate data on the area harvested.

Equations for the 'rest of the world' acreage were investigated, but no formulation tried yielded a significant price coefficient. It is likely that aggregation over the very dissimilar producing areas, and the need to use a price deflated by a world index, introduce too strong a specification error to be overcome. Accordingly, for the rest of the world, including Nigeria, the acreage decision is assumed to be exogenous.

The estimated long-run elasticities of the effects of prices on area harvested range from 0.24 for Cameroon, 0.27 for Brazil, and 0.30 for Ghana to 3.78 for Indonesia, 5.77 for Côte d'Ivoire, and 6.13 for Malaysia. The long run refers not only to the lag between prices and the response of harvested area, but also to the impact of the lagged dependent variable, which implies a partial adjustment around this long lag, thus capturing the effect of a longer history of prices.

The high elasticities for Côte d'Ivoire, Indonesia, and Malaysia are an expected result for the period under question, as area harvested rose very sharply at the beginning of the period to a substantial share of the world market within twenty years. When the real price is the only variable to be used, then the elasticity must be very high for the period covered. It would, however, be wrong to extrapolate very far on the basis of such elasticities without careful analysis of individual cases. The supply of suitable land might become a restraining factor, as might a reluctance to become too dependent on the cocoa market. Previous studies have not presented elasticities for the new producers (Malaysia and Indonesia) so that no comparisons are available. For the mature producers the elasticities are generally similar to those in earlier studies except for Côte d'Ivoire, where the present study produces a large value, while previous studies did not incorporate the recent period of very rapid growth.

In principle, the acreage and output equations can be combined to give a total long-run price elasticity. The percentage impact of prices on acreage can be combined with the elasticities of output with respect to acreage to give the impact of prices on output through acreage. This can be added to the

Table 7.3   *Long-run total elasticity of cocoa output with respect to price*

	e_{OP}	e_{OA}	e_{AP}	e_{OP}^{+}	e_{OP}^{*}
Cameroon	0	0.67	0.24	0.91	0.91
Côte d'Ivoire	0	1.28	5.77	7.39	7.39
Ghana	0.44	0.89	0.30	0.27	0.71
Indonesia	0	1.10	3.78	4.15	4.15
Malaysia	1.05	1.06	6.13	6.49	7.54
Brazil	0	1.14	0.27	0.30	0.30

Note: e_{OP} = elasticity of output harvested with respect to price; e_{OA} = elasticity of output with respect to acreage; e_{AP} = long-run elasticity of area with respect to price; e_{OP}^{+} = elasticity of output (net of harvesting effects) with respect to price (= $e_{OA} \cdot e_{AP}$); e_{OP}^{*} = total elasticity of output, including harvesting effects, with respect to price (= $e_{OP} + e_{OP}^{+}$).

Source: Section A.1.2

short-run impact of price on output for those countries in which such an effect was identified. The various elasticities are brought together in Table 7.3, using approximations which ignore interaction terms.

It can be seen that the elasticities of output with respect to acreage are all near unity, despite the fact that the models are linear, and hence not constrained to have unit elasticities. It is expected that a 1 per cent increase in area harvested would produce a near 1 per cent increase in output. If the marginal land is of lower quality, as may be the case in mature areas, such as Ghana and Cameroon, then the elasticity would be expected to be below unity. Values substantially larger than unity probably reflect the coincidence of better farming practices with the expansion of acreage.

The net elasticities of output with respect to price (e_{OP}^{+}) and the gross elasticities of output with respect to price (e_{OP}^{*}) both show the same picture. For those countries which are traditional producers and for which data are available, the estimated long-run price elasticites of supply are low; Ghana, Cameroon, and Brazil all have long-run price elasticities well below unity. For Nigeria, where the acreage figures are particularly suspect, all the rise in output must be attributed to prices and again the price elasticity was found to be very low.

Previous studies of the world cocoa market have not paid special attention to the new producers, the periods covered (finishing in the early 1980s) having missed the very large growth of output of three countries: Côte d'Ivoire, Malaysia, and Indonesia, which together accounted for almost one-half of world production by 1990. Any standard econometric model would impute very high price elasticities in all three cases, although the planting programmes were no doubt driven by the relative attractiveness of cocoa compared with specific alternatives, rather than with the general alternative as measured by the local cost of living index. Each of these countries would repay detailed study of the agronomic decision-making process involved. The high price-elasticities for these newer producers are crucially important for the cocoa market, since if their supply elasticities had been as low as those of the traditional producers then, given the growth of world income and the size of the price-elasticities of demand, the world market-clearing price of cocoa would certainly have been much higher.

7.3 THE DETERMINATION OF COCOA PRICES

The form of the model as structured has three layers of prices. Firstly, there are the producer prices for cocoa in local currencies which, when deflated by the local cost of living index, give the real price impact on acreage and harvesting decisions. Secondly, there is the world market price for cocoa, which equates the world supply and demand for raw cocoa. Thirdly, there are consumer prices which are equal, in the simplest case, to the world market price expressed in local currency divided by the local retail price index.

The focal point is the world market price for cocoa which is determined as a market-clearing variable. The actual mechanism and equation are discussed below. From the world price, an identity is used to determine the real consumer price:

Real consumer price = (World price × exchange rate)/
Local consumer price

This could be regarded as an equation in logs with all coefficients equal to unity. As mentioned earlier in Section 7.1, the real price of products containing cocoa has a mark-up over the real price of cocoa. However, if this mark-up is constant it would appear merely in the intercept of the above identity. Since experiments with demand equations show a very close link to the real cocoa price, it was not thought necessary to construct separate behavioural equations for the real price in consuming countries.

The position of the producer price link to the world cocoa price is somewhat analogous. If there are free markets with constant mark-ups, then the producer price would also be linked to the world cocoa price. However, in producer countries the price received by farmers is sometimes controlled by the government and is not directly related to the world price and the exchange rate. Hence, it is necessary to estimate the links from the world price to the local price before the model can be closed by the market-clearing mechanism.

The relationship of local producer prices to world prices has been explained by Akiyama and Duncan, who related the log of the producer price in dollars to the log of the world price in dollars without any lags. This formulation imposes complete passing-on of exchange rate changes. The goodness of fit was around 80 per cent for four countries, while that for Brazil was 99 per cent. Groenendaal and Vingerhoets adopt the most disaggregated approach to prices: demand is related to the import unit value of cocoa in local currency, while production is related to producer prices in local currency. There are then three sets of price equations:

(a) import unit values in consumer countries are related to the world cocoa price times the exchange rate;
(b) export unit values for the producers in dollars are related to the world price;
(c) producer prices in local currency are related to export unit values times the exchange rate.

All equations included lagged independent and lagged dependent variables in order to allow partial adjustment of the various prices to each other.

A model of producer prices

In the present study, producer price equations for the seven main producing countries are constructed, all using the same approach. The 'rest of the world' sector uses the world spot price as an explanatory variable in supply, and so does not require a price linking equation.

Since the natural formulation of the link must be multiplicative (i.e. multiplying by the exchange rate), it is essential to estimate the equations in log-linear form. The dependent variable is the log of the nominal producer price while the central independent variables are the log of the exchange rate (local currency per $US) and the log of the Ghana spot price in $US. Two variants of this model are tried. Firstly, lagged adjustment is tested for by including lagged independent variables and the lagged dependent variable. This would pick up cases where the government controlled the price partly on the basis of the movement in world prices and exchange rates in previous years. The second variant is the introduction of a time trend which, in effect, allows the margin relative to the world price to increase (for a positive coefficient). Such a phenomenon might be caused by a quality differential which was valued more highly over time.

The equations, which are estimated for a period from the mid-1960s to 1990, are given in Section A.1.3. For all but Côte d'Ivoire and Cameroon the goodness of fit is extremely high. The long-run impact of exchange rate changes is, in these five cases, remarkably near unity, despite the equations being unconstrained. In most cases, the long-run coefficient on the world price is not unity, indicating that a 1 per cent change in world prices at a given exchange rate was not associated with a 1 per cent change in the producer price in local currency. Quality differentials, both between countries, and between exports and domestic production, are one reason why all cocoa prices do not move in step with the spot price of Ghana cocoa in London. The action of governments to control producer prices is clearly another important reason, which appears to have been paramount for Cameroon and Côte d'Ivoire. For example, the producer price in Côte d'Ivoire was held constant from the period 1985 until 1988, despite substantial variations in the world price of cocoa; the factors which led to this were domestic and not susceptible to econometric modelling.

These equations link the world price to local producer prices, for given exchange rates and local retail prices. The real prices of cocoa in consumer countries are linked by identities to the world price so that the one variable remaining to be explained is the world price level.

The determination of the world cocoa price

As indicated above, the world price acts as the link between producer prices and consumer prices. Once it is determined then individual market demands and supplies are determined through the price-linking equations.

The world market price is seen as a market-clearing price. However, there are important stocks of cocoa beans which vary from year to year and act as an extra source of supply. Hence two equations are needed to close the system. One is an identity relating demand, supply, and actual stock changes; the other is a price behaviour equation which relates prices to some function of available stocks to desired stocks.

Akiyama and Duncan equate the change in actual world stocks to the sum of all the world supplies in the year less all the demands (per capita times population). Groenendaal and Vingerhoets modify this by multiplying the total world supply by a factor of 0.99 to account for a transportation loss of 1 per cent. Since the latter assumption is embedded in the calculation of stocks by the ICCO, it is also used in the present study. In matching world supply of cocoa beans and world demand for cocoa products there are some other errors introduced by inaccuracies in the data. For example, not all countries are measured and consumer stock data are not available. All such errors are necessarily absorbed by the figures for producer stock changes. Provided the errors are fairly constant with respect to actual stock changes, this should not disturb the estimation of the world price equation which is based on the measured stock movements.

The determination of the world price is dealt with in rather different fashion by the two studies which have a fully articulated system. Akiyama and Duncan relate the real world price (US import unit value of cocoa deflated by a world import price index of all goods) to its own lagged value and to the ratio of end-of-period stocks to world grindings of cocoa during the period. The use of grindings, instead of final demand, necessitates the introduction of another equation relating grindings in the current year to demands in the current and previous years. The sign of the stocks/grindings ratio is negative, reflecting the argument that when actual stocks (or expected stocks) are especially high relative to desired stocks (which are related to the level of sales) then prices will be bid down as stocks are released. The introduction of the lagged dependent variable indicates that prices react to the stock/demand ratio with partial adjustment.

A more difficult issue is that of whether to work in real prices. The Akiyama–Duncan formulation suggests that for *given* supplies and demands, which have themselves been determined by real prices, the willingness to alter the world price for a given stock/sales ratio will be affected by movements in the general index of prices. This is also a controversial approach since it suggests that the desired stock level is a function not only of expected sales but of cocoa prices relative to other prices. There is a case that the interest rate should be important as measuring the cost of stockholding, and the general price index may be serving as a proxy for this effect.

Groenendaal and Vingerhoets formulate their model in nominal prices, introducing the general consumer price index as an explanatory variable linking cocoa to other markets, together with the lagged nominal price. The stock-adjustment terms are more complex than those of Akiyama and Duncan. The desired level of stocks is set equal to the average level for a twenty-year period, which is 30 per cent of current grindings. The difference between opening stocks and 30 per cent of the previous year's grindings is introduced as a variable expected to have a negative impact on nominal cocoa prices. The change in the difference relative to the level of grindings is also introduced, with a negative sign, to allow for changes in demand. This last term is of doubtful relevance since the stocks/grindings ratio allows for changes in demand.

Since the estimated equation is not reported in the study the importance of the various terms cannot be evaluated.

A model of world cocoa prices

The determination of the world cocoa price, which is expressed in $US for Ghanaian cocoa in the London market, has three elements. The price, which is in nominal terms, is related to the ratio of the end-of-year total stock levels (free stocks plus buffer stocks) to the world grindings of that year, to the world consumer price index, and to the lagged (one year) price of cocoa.

The stocks/grindings ratio expresses the extent to which cumulated excess of supply over demand will depress the price. The deflation by grindings, which serves to scale the measure of the excess supply to the size of the market, replaces deflation by total world consumption in order to come into line with previous studies (there are also problems in obtaining world consumption figures for the years 1974 and 1975 after which time the ICCO replaced the FAO as the collection agency for data). It is expected that this ratio will have a negative effect on prices.

The nominal price of cocoa is related to the general consumer price index in order to allow for some measure of opportunity costs. The higher the consumer price index the more is forgone in nominal terms by holding cocoa stocks. The impact is thus expected to be positive. The lagged dependent variable allows for partial adjustment of the nominal cocoa price to changes in the cocoa market. It, too, is expected to have a positive sign.

The whole equation is estimated in log form, after some experiments, and is reported in Section A.1.3. The goodness of fit with an R^2 of 92 per cent is satisfactory for an equation where the dependent variable is not trend-dominated. The short-run elasticities are both substantial: a 1 per cent increase in world consumer prices raises the world cocoa price by 0.3 per cent in the first year (ignoring any effects such a change would also have on world supply and demand), while an *ex post* increase of 1 per cent in the stocks/grindings ratio will lower the world price by 0.9 per cent. In the long run such effects will be much greater since the coefficient of the lagged dependent variable is substantially greater than zero, but it is not meaningful to attempt such calculations without allowing for the feedbacks through world supply and demand.

In order to close the model it is necessary to link world grindings to world consumption for those years where there are data. Experiments reveal that there appears to be a structural break between FAO data for the pre-1974 period and ICCO data for 1976 onwards. Accordingly, the equation is fitted solely to the period 1975–90. Akiyama and Duncan related grindings to current and past world consumption, but for this later period there was no evidence for the presence of the lagged term. The simple linear linking equation, which has an R^2 of 0.99, is included in Section A.1.3.

Two identities are introduced to close the model. In the first, the net world crop is equated to world grindings *plus* total closing stock *less* total opening stock. Since the world grindings series is already endogenous, being a function of world consumption, which is the sum of the individual consumption sectors, and the net world crop is also endogenous, the impact is to make closing stocks endogenous. These will adjust, given supply and demand, so that the price producing these supplies and demands bears the relation to the stocks/grindings variable implied by the price equation.

The second identity is one which partitions total world stocks into free stocks plus ICCO buffer stocks. The latter term is taken to be exogenous, depending on policy choice, so that free stocks become endogenous. These two identities plus those relating world gross crop and world consumption to their component parts are also shown in Section A.1.3.

ANNEXE

The Demand for Chocolate and the Demand for Cocoa

As already explained, past econometric studies of the demand for cocoa have treated it as an item of final consumption, though in fact it is an input into various chocolate products, including chocolate confectionery and chocolate biscuits etc. In the UK, for example, it was estimated in 1988 that 480,000 tonnes of chocolate products were consumed while 140,000 tonnes of cocoa were used to make those products. The ratio of the volume of cocoa to the volume of chocolate products fluctuated between 25 per cent and 39 per cent during the period 1961 to 1990 (UNCTAD/ICCO, 1991). Correspondingly the price of chocolate products per tonne at retail in 1988 was £4,784 (nominal terms) with a wholesale price of £3,145 a tonne, while the UK import unit value of cocoa was £1,140 and the spot price of Ghana cocoa in London was £1,146.

The differences in these prices indicate that there were several other factors influencing the price, and hence the demand, for chocolate. Variations in chocolate demand driven by such factors will affect the derived demand for cocoa. Ideally a complete model of the chocolate-manufacturing decision process and the demand for chocolate should be constructed. However, with lack of data on the inputs into the final products, this is not possible.

The purpose of this Annexe is to explore the modelling of the demand for chocolate, since this is the product involved in household consumption decisions, and then to establish equations linking the volume of chocolate to the volume of cocoa and the price of chocolate to the price of cocoa. Such a system would provide the means of linking genuine final demand equations to a world supply—demand system for cocoa. The model, which consists of several behavioural equations and identities, has been applied to UK data for illustrative purposes.

The demand for chocolate goods

Although chocolate is sold in a wide variety of forms it is necessary to treat it as a homogeneous product because of data limitations. Changes in the composition of demand (e.g. with respect to the amount of cocoa used per physical unit of output) are thus not directly captured. In so far as such changes are reflected in the final price, and there are not strong variations in the demand for the product depending solely on its quality (as measured by the input composition), then a straightforward demand equation will be appropriate.

Demand is most easily treated as a per capita relationship—growth in the population will thus lead, *ceteris paribus*, to a proportionate rise in demand. This implicitly assumes that the age structure of the population does not affect total demand. In most countries the age structure changes sufficiently slowly, that only very large differences in the demand functions by age-group would be reflected in identifiable shifts in aggregate demand.

The standard model of the final demand per capita for chocolate can be hypothesized to be of the form:

$$ch = f(Y/N, RCHP, RELP), \tag{1}$$

where ch is the quantity of chocolate products purchased per capita; N is the population; Y is a measure of real income; $RCHP$ is the real retail price of chocolate products; and $RELP$ is the relative price of chocolate to sugar confectionery.

This model specification is linked to the total volume of chocolate products by the identity:

$$ch = CHQ/N \tag{2}$$

where CHQ is the total volume of chocolate products consumed.

As well as the final price of chocolate products, which allows for general substitution against other consumer goods, it is sensible to include prices of close substitutes. A series for sugar confectionery prices is available and this is included in the form of the relative price of chocolate products to sugar products ($RELP$). The own-price and cross-price variables are linked to the nominal price of chocolate products by the identities:

$$RCHP = CHP/RETP \tag{3}$$

$$RELP = CHP/SUGP, \tag{4}$$

where *RETP* is the retail price index; *SUGP* is the final price of sugar products; and *CHP* is the final price of chocolate products.

A further modelling issue must be confronted. Several studies have found evidence of partial adjustment in the demand for cocoa with short-run elasticities somewhat lower than long-run elasticities. In a pure demand equation such lags are likely to be caused by habit persistence since, for a repeat purchase item, consumers will soon be aware of changes in prices. Gradual changes in tastes may also give the appearance of dynamic adjustment. Experiments with lags on prices, incomes, and the per capita consumption of chocolate were therefore explored.

The use of cocoa in chocolate goods

The second behavioural equation relates the use of cocoa to the final consumption of chocolate products. This equation is cast in a ratio form where the dependent variable (*RATIO*) is identically equal to the final consumption of cocoa divided by the final consumption of chocolate products in the same period:

$$RATIO = COQ/CHQ \tag{5}$$

where *COQ* is the final quantity of cocoa consumed in the economy.

This ratio is seen as being determined by the technical possibilities of chocolate product manufacture and the prices of the various inputs. Many inputs are used in the manufacture of chocolate products but there is no systematic volume or price data available on a time-series basis. The prices of raw cocoa and raw sugar are available and these enter the equation. It would be desirable to include the price of various vegetable oils (soya was found to be significant by Behrman), but only rather short time-series are available on a consistent basis. Without a detailed technical specification it is not clear whether sugar and cocoa are substitutes or complements in the manufacture of chocolate products (sugar confectionery is expected to be a substitute for final chocolate demand), and hence there is no a priori restriction on the sign of the sugar price in this equation.

The question of a general price deflator in the input choice equation is problematical. Such a deflator should measure the prices of all other inputs in *that process*. The effects of prices elsewhere will be caught in the demand equations. One solution is to use the prices of inputs deflated by the output price since this encapsulates the weighted effects of all inputs. In this case, the output price is the wholesale price of chocolate. An alternative is to use the general retail price index (wholesale price index) as a reflection of all costs in the economy.

The form of the cocoa use equation is thus of the form:

$$RATIO = f(copr/wchp, rsugpr/wchp \ldots) , \qquad (6)$$

where *copr* is the price of raw cocoa; *rsugpr* is the price of raw sugar; and *wchp* is the wholesale price of chocolate products.

The two price variables in effect introduce two further identities into the system. The equation can include lags in order to allow for partial adjustment of the manufacturing process to input prices. A time trend can also be introduced in linear or log-linear form to allow for gradual changes in product specifications due to habit changes or marketing strategies. For the input prices there are two types of price series available. It is possible to consider either the UK import unit values or the spot prices of a particular quality of the inputs in the London market. Input unit values are likely to fluctuate less than the price for any particular type of cocoa as users substitute away from the temporarily more expensive qualities. Presumably there is a trade-off between saving on input costs and losing demand as the quality of the product falls, but this could be identified only with disaggregated data.

Price structure equations

Three separate levels of prices have been introduced into the model. Consumers are affected by the real retail price of chocolate, while the use of cocoa is determined by cocoa prices and the wholesale price of chocolate. Cocoa is itself a major component of the wholesale chocolate price. Hence for a single market, where the price of cocoa can be taken as given, it is necessary to have equations linking the wholesale chocolate price to the raw cocoa price, and the retail chocolate price to the wholesale chocolate price. The equations allow for partial adjustment by the inclusion of the lagged dependent variable. The link between the retail price of chocolate and the wholesale price of chocolate depends on taxation and on the distribution mark-up. Data for earlier years published by the UK Chocolate Manufacturers' Association suggests that the mark-up was very stable. The equation is of the form:

$$CHP = f(wchp) \qquad (7)$$

For the link between the wholesale price of chocolate and the price of cocoa some allowance must be made for the prices of other inputs. With data available on the raw sugar price the equation is of the form:

$$wchp = f(copr, rsugpr, retpr), \qquad (8)$$

where the retail price stands as an index of all other prices. It can be seen that these prices affect both the price of chocolate and possibly the amount of cocoa used in chocolate manufacture.

For the system of equations the exogenous variables are the total population, real income, the retail price index, the price of sugar confectionery, the price of raw cocoa, and the price of raw sugar. The endogenous variables are the wholesale price of chocolate, the retail price of chocolate, the ratio of cocoa to chocolate in chocolate products, the per capita demand for chocolate, the total demand for chocolate, the total demand for cocoa, the real final price of chocolate products, and the relative price of chocolate to sugar products.

Estimation of the demand system

Data are taken from a number of sources. The prices and final consumption of chocolate and sugar confectionery are taken from the Confectionery Alliance *Annual Report*. The final consumption of cocoa is taken from the ICCO as is the spot (Ghana) price of cocoa. The macroeconomic data are taken from the IMF annual *International Financial Statistics*. The price of raw sugar is taken from the *Annual Report* of the International Sugar Council. Data relate to the period 1964–90. The results of ordinary least squares regressions are shown below (*t* values in brackets):

(1) *Per capita chocolate demand*

$$CH = 3.87 + 0.632(Y/N) - 0.080\ RCHP + 0.430\ CH(-1)$$
$$\quad\ (4.56)\ (4.88) \qquad\quad (4.83) \qquad\qquad (3.52)$$

$R^2 = 0.956$

(2) *Ratio of volume of cocoa to volume of chocolate*

$$RATIO = 0.085 - 0.037(copr/wchp) + 0.808\ RATIO(-1)$$
$$\qquad\quad\ (2.72)\quad (2.82) \qquad\qquad\qquad (9.33)$$

$R^2 = 0.824$

(3) *Retail chocolate price*

$$CHP = -13.44 + 1.153\ wchp + 0.255\ CHP(-1)$$
$$\qquad\ (0.96)\ (19.66) \qquad (6.45)$$

$R^2 = 0.999$

(4) *Wholesale chocolate price*

$$wchpr = 14.477 + 0.155\ spotpr(-1) + 0.345\ Sugrpr(-1)$$
$$\qquad\quad\ (0.617)\ (5.941) \qquad\qquad (2.030)$$
$$\qquad\quad + 1.329\ Retpr + 0.516\ wchpr(-1)$$
$$\qquad\qquad\ (3.364) \qquad\quad (3.874)$$

$R^2 = 0.997$

The system was re-estimated by Zellner's seemingly unrelated regressions method but the results were very similar, suggesting that there is little correlation between the errors of different equations. Given that there is no simultaneity between this set of equations, the fact that they are recursive and the inter-equation error covariances are low, it appears that ordinary least squares will be a reliable technique of estimation.

Some comments on the coefficients are in order. In the chocolate demand equation the price of sugar confectionery was insignificant, as were lagged values of the chocolate price and income. All the coefficients had the expected sign and the relatively low value on the lagged dependent variable suggested a fairly rapid adjustment to changing circumstances. The equation for the use of cocoa in chocolate manufacturing found no evidence that this was affected by the price of raw sugar, suggesting that there is little substitutability between these two inputs. The cocoa price itself was significant, suggesting that other inputs are substitutable for cocoa when its price rises. The coefficient on the lagged dependent variable was high, implying slower adjustment to changes in the relative price of inputs. The equation for the retail price of chocolate showed a very close fit to the wholesale price, and the low coefficient on the lagged dependent variable supported the hypothesis of rapid adjustment to changes in the wholesale price. Finally, the wholesale price of chocolate was also strongly correlated with the raw cocoa and sugar prices and the high coefficient on the lagged dependent variable suggested a slow speed of adjustment to changes in input costs.

These equations can be used to derive a relationship between the demand for cocoa and the exogenous variables. Given the presence of the lagged dependent variables both short- and long-run impacts are involved. Because of the ratio equation, which introduces a non-linearity into the system, the reduced-form equation is itself non-linear.

Income and raw cocoa prices have quite different impacts on the demand for cocoa. A change in income affects the demand for chocolate according to the first equation. There are no other links in the system, so the demand for cocoa responds proportionately because nothing has changed which affects the ratio of the use of cocoa to chocolate. A price change of raw cocoa affects the wholesale price, which in turn affects the retail price. At the same time, the change in the wholesale price affects the ratio of cocoa to chocolate, while the change in the retail price affects the demand for chocolate. A higher price thus reduces the demand for chocolate and simultaneously leads to a lower use of cocoa in chocolate manufacture—the effects reinforce each other to produce a fall in the demand for cocoa. In the long run, the gradual adjustment of the system will increase prices further and reduce the demand for cocoa further.

Conventionally the impact of changes in explanatory variables on a dependent variable is measured by elasticities (the percentage change in the response relative to the percentage change in the impulse variable). For a single equation in double-log form the elasticity is the coefficient of the impulse variable but in a system which is a mixture of linear and non-linear equations linked by non-linear identities, no simple formula can be obtained. The elasticity has to be obtained by solving for the reduced form at two values of the impulse variable and approximating the point elasticity by a calculation based on small finite changes. As pointed out above, the results will in general depend on the level of all the variables at which the evaluation is made.

An alternative equation is given by the reduced-form approach in which the per capita consumption of cocoa is related to real GDP per capita, the real spot price of cocoa (lagged by one period), and the lagged dependent variable (1962–90):

$$CONSPC = 0.666 + 0.0639(Y/N) - 0.0128\ RSPOTPR(-1)$$
$$(2.72)\quad (2.291)\qquad\quad (4.968)$$
$$+\ 0.649\ CONSPC(-1)$$
$$(6.589)$$

$$R^2 = 0.843$$

This equation can be used together with data on population to give forecasts for the total consumption of cocoa. The signs of the variables are as expected, and other variables (such as the sugar price) were not significant.

It is not possible to make a direct comparison of the two approaches, since the experiments with lags and with variables to be included mean that one is not a simple reflection of the other. The evaluation of short-run elasticities also depends crucially on the lag structure. For example, in the reduced-form model, the current price has no effect on demand so that the short-run price elasticity is zero. The long-run elasticities can, however, be compared. Given that both systems are dynamic, the calculation of a long-run elasticity starts from a hypothetical equilibrium value of the dependent variable(s) given (say) at the sample mean of the independent variables. A shift in the price or income variable is then traced through the system at its new equilibrium position and the percentage change between equilibria relative to the percentage change in the driving variable is calculated. For the mixed linear and non-linear system which is used to model the linked demands for chocolate and for cocoa this is equivalent to operating on the implicit long-run reduced form for the system which will be non-linear in variables such as price and income. For a medium-size (10 per cent) change in the spot price of cocoa (around its sample mean value of £1,017 per tonne) the reduced-form approach yielded an estimated long-run price elasticity of −0.29 while the system approach gave a value of −0.45. The long-run income elasticity for the reduced form (measured for a 10 per cent change around the mean value of real income) was 1.49. For the system approach, where income affects chocolate consumption, but without any impact on the ratio of cocoa use, the demand for cocoa changes proportionately and the long-run income elasticity is 0.91.

Conclusions

It is possible, where adequate data exist, to model the demand for cocoa via a system of equations relating to the final demand for chocolate, the use of cocoa in chocolate manufacture, and the ·relationship between the chocolate price and the cocoa price. Such a procedure is certainly preferable to that of modelling a demand for cocoa equation directly. For the UK it appears that it is possible to obtain satisfactory structural equations. The long-run elasticities given by the two approaches are fairly similar, but the system approach yields a higher price—and lower income—elasticity than the reduced-form approach. Further investigation for other countries would be needed to confirm whether this is a general tendency. Were these results to be more widespread then the policy implications would be important—the system approach would suggest a much slower growth of cocoa demand for a given income growth path, but would also suggest a bigger response to price changes caused by external shocks to the world supply–demand system.

8

The World Coffee Market

8.1 THE DEMAND FOR COFFEE

Coffee is a commodity with essentially a single final use, i.e. as a beverage. Furthermore, it is not combined with any other inputs to produce the final good, although it is subject to a variety of manufacturing processes to produce soluble products. These characteristics distinguish it from cocoa, where the use in chocolate and products using chocolate introduces the need to consider the input composition. For coffee, the price of the final product is related to the price of the raw material together with manufacturing and distribution costs.

A distinctive feature of coffee is the wide variety of qualities available. Not only are there two principal varieties of coffee bean, robusta and arabica, but each of these exists in several subvarieties. These command a wide range of price differentials depending on tastes in various consuming countries. Little systematic study of the demands for coffee variety has been incorporated into complete models of the world coffee market because of the lack of complete information on quantities and prices market by market. The study by Lord (1991) does address this issue for a subset of producers, but does not go as far as producing a full model with separately determined prices for all the different varieties.

Practical difficulties then make it necessary to treat coffee as a single homogeneous good, but the use of separately estimated demand equations for the main consuming countries does allow implicitly for some of the impact of different preferences for the various types of coffee. A further simplification has to be made in that the form in which the coffee is purchased (beans or soluble) is not distinguished, again because of lack of data.

The demand for coffee is treated as for any other good. The major determinants of per capita consumption are real per capita income and the real retail price of coffee. Empirical studies have suggested that habit is important in this market, so that there may be dynamic adjustment to changes in income or price. The issue of substitutes is also problematical. In some countries other hot beverages are seen as close substitutes (e.g. tea in the UK), while in others cold beverages, such as soft drinks, are the principal rivals (e.g. in the USA). The lack of price data for such substitutes and the need to consider each market separately has resulted in there being little econometric modelling of substitution in world coffee models. The lack of growth of coffee demand, while income has grown in some important markets (notably the USA), has also led to the need to consider models which allow for saturation or non-linear responses between income and demand. The functional forms used for the demand equations are likely to be more important than for cocoa, where the demand for chocolate does not appear to have reached saturation.

A feature of some interest has been the suggestion by some authors, see Vogelvang (1988), that the demand for coffee shows a degree of irreversibility against price changes. A high price leads to a loss of demand, which is not recaptured once prices fall back to their original level. It is difficult, however, to disentangle this phenomenon from the large changes in consumption that took place both after the war when coffee became plentiful and soluble coffee became common, and the large changes that took place after various price shocks.

A number of studies of coffee demand covering the major consumers have been made and the results of some more recent studies are briefly reviewed. A general point that has to be borne in mind is that data on consumption are not available generally, so that 'disappearance' is used. This is the level of net imports minus the change in wholesale stocks, which is equal to consumption plus the change in retail stocks. At times of rapid price movement stocks can change dramatically so that consumption can be mismeasured by disappearance.

(i) *Akiyama and Duncan (1982).* This study, using annual data for the period 1965 to 1979, relates per capita net imports to per capita real GDP and the real coffee price. The price is the world average price ($) divided by a local price deflator (it is unclear whether an exchange rate factor has been included). Lagged prices are also included so that there is a distinction between short- and long-run price elasticities. All variables are in logs so that the coefficients are equal to elasticities, which implies that no saturation or irreversibility effects were estimated. The coverage of countries employs some broad groupings so that the whole of the world is covered by the study. The estimated long-run income elasticity ranges from zero for the USA and Brazil to 1.99 for Japan, with the European Community at 0.60. The fact that no significant income elasticity could be found for the USA, the largest consuming country, was one striking result of this study. The estimated long-run price elasticities are generally small: −0.11 for the European Community, −0.37 for the USA and −0.40 for Japan, with a world average of −0.23. For many other countries, the use of the world price deflated by a local consumer price is a rather unsatisfactory way of measuring the retail price, and this may have affected the size of the price elasticities.

(ii) *Vogelvang (1988).* This study explicitly recognizes that disappearances include both consumption and changes in retail stocks. The consumption aspect is theoretically specified as a relation between per capita consumption and real prices and real per capita income. A semi-log relationship for income is postulated by taking the log of per capita income. To this a term to explain changes in stocks is added in the form of the change in the real price. This model is estimated on quarterly data for the period 1972–80 for ten countries. In the estimating form a different specification is used, which cannot be derived exactly from the theoretical model. The level of total disappearance is related to the population level, real prices, and the log of real per capita income as well as the change in real prices. There is no intercept in this form of the equation. The formulation appears to multiply the original by population but, by failing to multiply prices or per capita income, a hybrid form is obtained.

In fact, Vogelvang finds that in every case total disappearance is uncorrelated with per capita income, which is interpreted to mean that income plays no role in coffee demand. Since there is included a term in population (multiplying the original intercept) this may well pick up much of the effect due to the growth of income. Vogelvang, in fact, drops the per capita income variable before obtaining the final equation from which price elasticities are determined. This equation is linear in all variables so that elasticities are not constant. There are no lags in the equation so that demand is assumed to react fully (within the quarter) to all changes. The estimated price elasticities at the sample mean values range from -0.20 for West Germany to -0.79 for Japan, with ten out of fourteen countries having elasticities smaller than -0.40.

For the group of non-member ICO countries a separate equation is estimated on the basis of a sigmoid curve with respect to time, thus allowing for saturation. Since this contains neither income nor price variables no elasticities can be reported.

For the period covered, which is quite short relative to most annually based models, the price elasticities are remarkably similar. However, the omission of an income variable and the lack of dynamics, as well as the shortness of the period, means that these results cannot readily be accepted as a guide to price responsiveness in the 1980s.

(iii) *Akiyama and Varangis (1989)*. This later World Bank study, based on annual data for 1974–84, estimates separate demand equations for a much wider range of countries (twenty-nine in all). Again, the form of the model is double log, except for a handful of countries where a semi-log form is used to capture declining income elasticities (W. Germany, Italy, Netherlands, UK, Australia, Austria, and Japan). The price is measured by the local retail price deflated by a local consumer price index. The equations used do not introduce any lagged values so that complete adjustment within a year is assumed. The results indicate income elasticities below 0.5 for about one-half of the countries, of which a number— including the USA—are shown as having zero income elasticity. Almost one-half the countries covered have price elasticities between zero and −0.25, with most of the rest between −0.25 and −0.5.

The model treats demand in non-member countries of the International Coffee Organization as exogenous. An important group of countries are the net exporters. Since the quota can limit exports, their own demands play an important role in determining producer stocks. The lack of a domestic retail price variable for this group is particularly problematical since the quota can isolate their domestic price from the world price. The results show generally low price elasticities. For those countries where the income elasticities are high (Ireland and Japan) it is suggested that this is related to the growth from very low levels of consumption early in the period, so that a non-constant elasticity model would be appropriate.

An updated version of this paper was published by Akiyama and Varangis (1990), which did not alter the previous elasticities but did add a few more countries, mainly small. For the total group of non-ICO member developing countries the income elasticity is 0.50 and the price elasticity −0.09, while for the centrally planned economies (excluding China) the price elasticity is −0.22. The world price elasticity is estimated to be −0.33, with the income elasticity at 0.6. The authors compare this to previous estimates of the world price elasticity which had tended to be slightly lower at around −0.2, while the income elasticity was similar to previous studies. The difference in the price elasticity is attributed to the use of correct retail price data for the net importing countries.

(iv) *Lord (1991)*. The study by Lord, in which coffee is just one of the commodities analysed, is perhaps the most detailed undertaken to date. A distinguishing feature is the analysis of demand for coffee by type. The study focuses only on the Latin American producers and so is not a complete account of the world coffee market. Nevertheless, because each country of origin is identified as producing a different type of coffee, the results are not likely to be substantially distorted by this focus.

The demand equations are built in two stages. The first stage, for each importing country analysed, is an aggregate demand for coffee equation (total import demand). Imports are related to real income and to the average import price deflated by the general domestic price level. The equations are in double log form and an error correction model is used to allow for dynamic adjustment. The import price is defined as a weighted average (CES weighting) of the prices of the individual coffees imported—the weights are not determined by shares of total inputs, which is somewhat surprising.

The second stage of the analysis is to define a series of export demand functions which are the demands, by a given country, for the exports of each of its suppliers. Exports from a given supplier divided by total imports are assumed to be related to the price of the specific export relative to the general import price of coffee. The summation over all exports is made consistent by defining the export demand share for the residual supplier as one minus all the other export shares. For the case studied by Lord of Latin American exporters, this treatment of the rest of the world as a residual is acceptable, but the asymmetry would not be satisfactory in a global coffee model. In practice it is necessary that these 'share' equations all lie in the range zero to one, so a 'logistic'-type transform is used. By relating the individual export price to the average of all competitive prices, the model assumes an equal degree of substitutability between different coffees. The export share equations are also estimated by an error correction model to allow for dynamic adjustments between sources of supply as well as to the general level of coffee demand.

The import price (weighted average of individual export prices from various suppliers) in each country is hypothesized also to be in a long-run proportional relationship to the world price. The world price is one which clears the aggregate supply–demand balance, given the demand for stocks.

The econometric results for this detailed model are based on annual data for the period 1960 to 1985. In order to identify individual country-to-country trade flows in coffee, UN data were utilized. This presents some difficulty in matching aggregate demand to aggregate supply, since the latter is taken from a different source. The results for import demand (total consumption of coffee) show rapid adjustment to equilibrium. The long-run income elasticities for total demand in the main consuming countries for Latin American coffee are almost all less than 1.2, including a positive elasticity (0.2) for the USA, this last being in distinct contrast to other studies, and may be due to the different data period and to the use of lagged adjustment terms in the error correction mechanism. The long-run price elasticities for total coffee demand are mostly −0.2 or less.

The second stage of the model is the substitution between the different sources of supply to meet a given coffee demand. The price elasticity in this equation is related to the elasticity of substitution, which measures the percentage change in relative quantities purchased brought about by a 1 per cent change in relative prices. The long-run elasticities of substitution for the various Latin American countries covered in this study vary substantially, from less than −2.0 for Ecuador, Haiti, and Mexico to over −4.0 for Costa Rica and over −5.0 for Honduras. For Brazil, the corresponding elasticity is −2.1. These are calculated by taking, for example, the elasticities of Brazilian coffee versus all other coffee in each of the separate importing markets and constructing a weighted average. The short-run elasticities are much lower, suggesting that importers take time to switch their preferences as relative prices shift. Were all coffees to be seen by consumers to be completely substitutable, then the elasticities of substitution would all be very high—low values imply some specific preference for a given supplier that requires a large price differential to overcome.

Although this model is best seen as a model of the market for Latin American coffees, it does show how a much more detailed approach to commodity modelling can be undertaken which allows for product heterogeneity. Differences in supply conditions and in consumer tastes can thus be allowed for, if country-to-country trade data can be obtained.

(v) *Yeboah (1992)*. This study uses annual data for a period from 1960 to 1988, where possible (some countries were analysed from 1970 onwards). Two differences from earlier studies are incorporated. Firstly, the price of substitute beverages is included (tea or cocoa), but tea emerges as a complement while cocoa is a substitute in those cases where the coefficients are significant. A second new variable is the proportion of the population aged between 15 and 65 years—the basis for this is that younger people are known to drink less coffee. Where the proportion in this group changes, then total per capita consumption should change. The general functional form is double log so that all coefficients are elasticities. There is no attempt to allow for saturation and all the equations are static. The measurement of the price variables is not explicit but it appears that the study experimented with dollar prices of various coffees. The 'other mild' arabica price was the preferred series. The study appears not to convert world prices into domestic currency nor to deflate them by a local cost of living index, which would mean that the estimated price elasticity is likely to be substantially different from one based on retail prices.

The resulting estimates of price elasticities are substantially lower than in other studies, while for some countries (USA, Canada, Australia, New Zealand, and Brazil) the estimated income elasticities are negative. The potential mismeasurement of the price variable may well account for the low price elasticities, while the negative income elasticities may be related to the inclusion of early years when demand was quite different. The variable relating to the proportion of adults in the 15 to 65 age-range was generally not significant, probably because it tends to change rather slowly at a country level. The prices of other beverages also were only occasionally significant, but these too would have suffered from mismeasurement.

This review of some of the most recent studies of the demand for coffee at a world level shows considerable divergence in the detail of the models used. Four issues need some further consideration:

   (i) the measurement of the price variable;
  (ii) the functional form of the demand relationship;
 (iii) the treatment of dynamic adjustment;
 (iv) the treatment of quality differentials.

It appears that there is now consensus on the price variable to be used—it should be the local retail price of coffee divided by the general consumer price index. This picks up the impact of exchange rate changes and the margin of retail prices over the cost of imported coffee. Only where such data are unavailable will a proxy need to be used.

The issue of functional form of the demand equation has received little detailed analysis, although several authors refer to aspects such as income elasticities which decline as income rises. The almost universal finding, that USA demand is not income-responsive, makes this an important problem to resolve. The key to this topic may well be the fact that the per capita consumption of coffee is likely to have a fairly strongly marked saturation level—people do not increase their consumption beyond a certain point, unlike the consumption of certain goods which do not have to be physically consumed. There are substantial differences in per capita consumption levels between countries, and it is likely that the saturation level will vary between countries depending on climate and custom. The use of constant elasticity models is thus likely to pose estimation problems: income has increased greatly during the period, while the real price of coffee has fallen greatly in recent years. Any model imposing constant elasticity to a variable which cannot respond very greatly will impute low elasticity values. Thus for coffee, as opposed to cocoa where the ability to eat chocolate bars is well above the level typically consumed, it is important to consider functional forms which allow for saturation.

These studies do not reach a strong conclusion on the speed of adjustment of demand to changes in income and price. There is some evidence that there may be a short lag and also limited evidence that disappearance may be related to changes in price through speculative effects on retail stocks.

Although Lord has shown how to take quality differentials into account, the method is too demanding on data to be used in the present study of the world coffee market—reconciling trade flow data with world production and stock data on a lengthy time-series basis would in itself be a major exercise. Were such data to be available, then Lord's approach would be capable of answering more detailed questions of policy for individual producing countries.

Present study

Demand equations are established for the largest consuming countries, including one producing country, Brazil. Data are available on a consistent basis only for ICA members so that the consumption of non-members is not specifically covered. The consumption of other producing countries and other member non-producing countries is aggregated into a 'rest of the world' variable. The former socialist countries of Eastern Europe and the Soviet Union also have to be excluded because of lack of data. Detailed data, produced by the ICO, on retail prices exist only from 1975, which becomes the earliest starting-point for this study.

The basic form of the equations tried was similar to those of earlier studies. Per capita consumption was related to per capita real income and the real retail price (retail coffee price deflated by the general retail price index). Lags on both variables as well as on the dependent variable were tried. In general it appeared that demand has adjusted rapidly so that there are no lags. The equations were also estimated in both linear and log-linear form, with the former being preferred. Some experiments on saturation were tried but there was little support for this. The USA, having experienced a very large fall in demand in the mid–1970s, has since experienced slow growth, which does not appear saturated. In some countries a time trend has been successfully introduced.

The major problem with this equation is the measurement of the dependent variable. The 'disappearance' of coffee in a country includes changes in retail stocks. Such a variable can be quite different between years, thus producing a rather irregular appearance to the dependent variable. An attempt was made to capture this effect by including the change in real prices, as in the work of Vogelvang, to pick up the determinants of the change in stocks, but in most cases this variable was insignificant.

The preferred equations are shown in section A.2.1. In most cases the income and price terms are significant and of the correct sign, while there is little evidence of partial adjustment. The elasticities (evaluated at means) of price

Table 8.1 *Long-run price and income elasticities of demand for coffee*

	Price	Income		Price	Income
USA	−0.10	0.46	Spain	−0.16	1.55
France	0	1.65	UK	−0.27	0.33
Germany, Fed. Rep.	−0.18	1.93	Japan	−0.29	1.37
Italy	−0.13	0.51	Brazil	−0.07	0.10
Netherlands	−0.28	0.70			

Source: Section A.2.1

and income are shown in Table 8.1. The price elasticities, which are low in every case, are similar to those found by Akiyama and Varangis, even though including six years not available to the earlier study. The income elasticities appear rather higher than before (except for Japan), perhaps reflecting the substantial increase in consumption at the end of the 1980s. Adding the predicted values of these nine countries together, which account for around 70 per cent of ICO member country consumption, and comparing them with the actual values, gives a squared correlation of 91 per cent.

The identifiable consumption of other member producers and consumers has remained fairly constant between the late 1970s and 1990, so that its treatment as an exogenous variable is not too damaging (the consumption of the nine increased by around 30 per cent during the same period). The fitted value for world consumption is built up out of this substantial but rather unvarying exogenous component and the predicted endogenous share, and has a correlation with the actual of 83 per cent, with an average error of about 2 per cent of the mean of world consumption during this period.

8.2 THE PRODUCTION OF COFFEE

The modelling of the supply of coffee is very similar to that for cocoa. Coffee is a tree crop in which there is a considerable lag between decisions to plant more trees and the output of more coffee. In the short run prices or other variables cannot affect the number of bearing trees (unless some are destroyed). However, variations in cultivation intensity could be affected by price movements, so that there could be a low short-run price-elasticity.

Studies of the production of coffee have not only stressed the lag structure of prices, created by the nature of the tree crop, but have also emphasized two other aspects of production. Firstly, there has been some evidence of a two-year bearing cycle, a heavy crop one year being followed by a lighter crop the following year. However, aggregation of a whole country's production tends to smooth out this pattern which is well established at a micro-economic level. The second factor, which appears especially important in the case of coffee, is the impact of the weather. A frost in Brazil not only cuts current output, but also damages the trees for more than one year so that output recovers only slowly. The severity of frosts in Brazil and the fact that they are not rare events means that the production side of any world coffee model will be subject to very powerful shocks—these can be explained *ex post* but not forecast. For *ex post* simulation analysis it is assumed that the same shock would have occurred. This does raise the problem, dealt with later, of whether to simulate excluding a variable to explain the shock or whether to include such a (dummy) variable. If such a variable is excluded the estimated model (before simulating alternative policies) will fail to pick up the effects of the shock on prices, so that the impact of the simulation must not be measured against actual prices but against forecast prices.

Some previous models of coffee production

The modelling of coffee production has attracted a number of studies, many of which are now very out of date. In addition, the operation of the International Coffee Agreements, which controlled exports going into the world market while the Agreements' economic clauses were in operation, has lessened the interest in modelling the production decision.

(i) *Akiyama and Duncan* (1982). This study estimates simple production functions for five countries and for the rest of the world, using annual data for the period 1963–79. Production is related to lagged production and to the producer price of coffee (or world price) deflated by a local cost of living index.

It is not clear whether the world price is converted into local currency. For Brazil, separate tree stocks and production equations are estimated. Tree stocks (not acreage) are related to their own lagged values and to deflated world prices. Production is related to lagged production, to tree stocks, and to the real producer price. A single dummy variable for years affected by frost is also introduced (implying that output lost was equal for 1964, 1970, and 1976).

For the major coffee-producing countries, the short-term price elasticities of production are generally relatively small (for Brazil and Colombia, the elasticities are 0.09 and 0.07 respectively). A short-run price elasticity for world coffee production is estimated at 0.12. The corresponding long-run elasticities are all substantial, with both Brazil and Colombia having values in the region of 1.0, with an estimated world elasticity of 0.74. The results are to be interpreted cautiously since producer price data were not available for some countries. Also, the lack of an explicit feedback through the stock of trees, and the shortness of lags on dependent variables in these equations, may mean that the full long-term impact is not captured. Smuggling may also be important—if the price is lower than that of a neighbouring country then *recorded* production will decline.

(ii) *Akiyama and Varangis* (1989). This study had access to a much fuller data set so that for eleven countries separate planting and production equations are estimated, while for another fifteen countries/regions simple production equations are fitted. The data are annual for 1968–86.

Where new planting equations can be estimated, these are related to real farmgate prices (possibly lagged). Production capacity is related to new and past plantings and production is modelled as a function of capacity, real farmgate prices, weather indices, and the previous year's output (to capture the biennial yield cycle).

Combining planting and production equations, supply-elasticities with respect to price were calculated by simulating the operation of the model. For the short-run (two-year) price-elasticities of supply, apart from Côte d'Ivoire, for which the estimated elasticity (0.55) was exceptionally high, the mean unweighted elasticity for all the other producing countries was very low (only 0.09). For the longer-run (ten-year) elasticities, the estimates are generally much lower than those found by Akiyama and Duncan. This difference may be due to the difference in price series and the difference in the period covered.

(iii) *Lord* (1991). The model by Lord is quite different from other studies on the production side, as well as on the demand side. Because each producer has some market power the model aims to determine exports from one country to another, so that in equilibrium the supply and demand for each trade flow is equal. Hence exports and not production are modelled. This evades problems caused where the difference between domestic production and exports does not all go into domestic consumption. Stock level changes in producer countries may well affect the world price.

By modelling export supply the study does not attempt to include the stock of trees directly; instead, lagged prices and lagged dependent variables produce a reaction to past values. The equations are in double log form based on the period 1960–85, and lags of up to nine or ten periods were used in prices. One distinct feature of Lord's approach is that prices are set as real dollar earnings since the object is taken as the acquisition of foreign currency. The deflator of the country's coffee export price to a particular consumer is a weighted average of local capital and labour prices. Export supply is also related to a trend variable to allow for changes in production and export processes. Estimates of the short-run export supply-elasticities for each producing country averaged over destinations ranged from an extremely low value for Brazil (0.01) to over 0.3 for a number of Central American countries. The unweighted mean of all the countries covered was 0.18.

A substantial problem with Lord's general approach, when applied to the case of coffee, is that it takes no account of the ICAs and the export quota system. For many of the years during the period modelled countries were bound to an export level determined by the commodity agreement. Modelling exports as if they were determined by long-run supply factors (lagged prices to pick up planting effects) is therefore not satisfactory.

The price-elasticities, although low in the short run, are very substantial in the long run. This may be due to the longer price lags used than in other studies as well as to the completely different price used—a dollar export price deflated by a domestic cost of living index (not converted into dollars). Lord also provides values of the *mean* lag of exports behind price. This is generally in the range seven to nine years indicating a very lengthy period before the supply side fully adjusts to price changes.

Finally, it should be noted that for countries, such as Côte d'Ivoire, where the government fixed the producer prices, there cannot be the usual link between world prices (lagged) and exports (regarded as a proxy for production). Domestic supply will be unaffected by world prices and if exports respond to world prices it would be without any lag.

The very special focus of this study makes it difficult to compare with earlier work, but it does confirm that there appears to be a feedback in the world coffee market through prices to supply.

Present study

The present study treats the output and planted area of coffee by separate equations. The former is seen as a short-run harvesting decision, constrained by the area of mature bushes, while the latter is an investment decision. The existence of export quotas implies that each producer will find it possible to sell only a given amount of coffee on the world market, any surplus production having to be sold to the domestic market, or stockpiled against future opportunities, or sold to non-ICA members. All of these opportunities are likely to command lower prices, so that the local producer price may reflect a weighted average of these different markets.

Output equations

Output equations are estimated for the eight largest producing countries for which there were data available, these countries accounting for about two-thirds of total ICO-member production. The data cover the period 1967 to 1990 for most countries.

The primary economic variable explaining output is the area harvested, since this must reflect the maximum potential output. In addition, a real producer price is included (producer price in local currency deflated by the local cost of living index) to capture opportunity costs of the work involved in harvesting, as well as the value of the crop. Experiments with short lags on prices were carried out in order to test for the possibility that farmers based decisions on earlier experience rather than the (possibly) unknown current year's price.

A lagged output variable was also included in order to check for a relationship between successive years. Such a relationship would be negative if the two-year yield cycle were dominant at the aggregate level. Finally, a time trend was included in order to allow for trends in productivity. Where the average age of the stock of trees was increasing, or the quality of trees or husbandry was declining, then the trend would be expected to be negative. An increasing proportion of high-yielding varieties coming into bearing would produce a positive trend.

The detailed equations are given in Section A.2.2(a). In every case the area variable is correlated with output, but real prices are significant only for Brazil and for Côte d'Ivoire, with elasticities of 0.18 and 1.07, respectively. These results confirm findings of earlier studies that producer prices are strongly associated with output in Côte d'Ivoire.

Lagged values of prices and of the output variable were found to be generally insignificant, and a negative time trend of a small magnitude was identified as significant for Brazil and Uganda. The goodness of fit of the equations was not very high, and this probably reflects the importance of variations in weather conditions affecting yearly output levels.

As a check on the goodness of fit of the output equations, the fitted values of the sum of the eight producers were regressed on the sum of the actual output. The squared correlation (1974–90) was 81 per cent and the equation reveals an intercept not significantly different from zero and a slope not significantly different from unity, thus indicating that there was no systematic bias in the output equations.

Adding in the production of all other ICO members treated as exogenous, and correlating this with the actual total output of ICO members, produced a squared correlation of 89 per cent.

Acreage equations

The acreage equations, which relate the area harvested to lagged prices, are seen as long-run investment equations. Ideally, a distributed lag distribution of past prices should be used, with the shortest lag representing the time it takes for a newly planted bush to its first yield crop. In practice, only a single lag on the real producer price variable has been found to be significant. Experiments on different lag lengths revealed that the significant lag lengths were different as between producers. In one case, that of Colombia, the only lag which appeared significant was three years, which is very short. In every case, a time trend was included to reveal the impacts of any determining variables (other than the real producer price) which were trended. Lack of data on other investment costs meant that more sophisticated equations could not be used. In most cases, the time trends were fairly small (in relation to mean acreage), even though statistically significant (see Section A.2.2(b)).

The goodness of fit of the acreage equations was rather variable—the equations for Brazil, Indonesia, and India all fitted very well, but those for Colombia, Mexico, and Guatemala fitted rather weakly. For the Côte d'Ivoire and for Uganda (for which output equations were estimated) there was not a long enough run of prices to fit the long lags required by the acreage equations.

The long-run elasticities of acreage with respect to real producer prices (evaluated at mean values) are 0.07 and 0.04 for Brazil and Colombia respectively, the two largest producers, 0.14 for Mexico, 0.08 for Guatemala, 0.07 for Indonesia, and 0.05 for India. These values are all strikingly low and, coupled with the lack of significant output price elasticities, suggest that supply responds little to changes in producer prices. However this is not altogether surprising given the lengthy period of export quotas. If it is recognized by farmers that the amount sold to ICA members will be strictly controlled, then there is little point in responding strongly to prices unless the domestic market is buoyant, or it is easy to sell to the non-ICO member countries.

8.3 PRICES AND MARKET-CLEARING

The world coffee market has functioned quite differently from the world cocoa market in that there have been quotas set on coffee exports for some but not all years included in the present analysis. When quotas have been in operation, ICO-producer members have agreed to limit their exports in a year to consumer members to a certain quota figure. This presents a large number of difficulties for econometric modelling, several of which have not been surmounted.

The first issue is the endogeneity of the quota. The ICA rules have been such that the quota has come into operation only at certain 'trigger prices'. The size of the quotas for individual countries also alter as the price passes further 'trigger' levels. Hence, as Vogelvang (1988) recognizes in the simulation part of his study (but not for that relating to estimation), the operation of the quota is endogenous to the model. Since the whole quota system has broken down and then been reformed later several times, it has been endogenous in a wider sense.

The second problem for econometric modelling reflects a real world difficulty for the system, namely that part of the market was not covered by the various coffee agreements. Coffee of member producers, surplus to quota exports and domestic consumption or stockbuilding, has been sold to non-members—thus driving down the price in this sector. Some arbitrage has also taken place between the two markets ('tourist' coffee) so that the price in the member market area is not determined just by direct quota sales. Without data on sales to non-member countries, and on the price in that market, it has not proved possible to model the non-market sector adequately.

Because of the presence of the quotas, which determine aggregate supply, the price-clearing mechanism has also been the subject of some variations in treatment, which are discussed below.

Retail prices

The price which affects final consumption is best taken to be the retail price of coffee (in local currency). Early studies (such as Akiyama and Duncan) used the world price of coffee deflated by a local cost of living index. This makes no allowance for local retail prices to move differently from the world price expressed in local currency. Akiyama and Varangis use the real retail price, as does Yeboah. This approach requires a link from retail prices in local currency to the world price. A double log equation is used in which the exchange rate is a second explanatory variable. Lags are used to test for partial adjustment in the passing on of costs.

The world price

The world price of coffee is usually taken to be one of the ICO 'indicator' prices. Akiyama and Duncan use an average of four types of coffee, while Akiyama and Varangis use the 'other milds' price. Vogelvang, who is concerned with short-term issues, uses the 'C' contract of the New York futures market, which concerns mainly 'other milds' coffee. All these prices are in dollars.

The key part of the model is the mechanism by which this price is assumed to be determined. In the Akiyama and Duncan study, which makes no reference to the operation of the quota system, the coffee price is deflated by an average cost of living index for the consuming countries. This 'real' price is assumed to be determined by the ratio of total world imports to total world stocks. No lags are introduced into the equation, but a dummy variable for 1976 and 1977 is used. Here consumer stocks are related to previous stocks, to world exports (imports) and to the ratio of the world coffee price to a general price index for agricultural commodities. The logic of this equation is somewhat less clear than the rest of the model since consumer stocks are likely to relate to opportunity costs in consuming, and not in producing, countries. The closing identity then makes producer stock changes endogenous, being what is needed to meet the difference between world production and the sum of world imports and consumption in producing countries. This model sees no constraint on exports—they are determined by domestic production less domestic consumption, both of which are endogenous and related to the world price.

Akiyama and Varangis explicitly recognize the existence of quotas. When the quotas are not operative their model takes the same approach as Akiyama and Duncan, i.e. that exports are endogenous, and hence react to world prices. During the quota period exports are taken as given, which implies that producer stocks become a residual. This, in turn, implies that the price in the producer markets can become decoupled from the world price if these stocks are unloaded on the domestic market, since arbitrage is no longer possible. Sales to non-member countries are also an outlet for such coffee and, were no resale possible between member and non-member countries, the price in this market could be expected to fall below the world market price. Without information on this market it will not be possible to give a complete picture of the workings of the world coffee market.

Producer prices

The link from the world price to the local producer price depends on the modelling of quotas. In the absence of any quotas the world price will be arbitraged to local producer prices, making allowance for exchange rates, domestic freight, taxes, etc. Akiyama and Duncan, in fact, use the world price in local currency as the equivalent to the producer price, while Akiyama and Varangis construct linking equations between local farmgate prices, the exchange rate, and world prices. Detailed equations are not given so it is not possible to determine the success of these equations, or whether they used lags to allow for partial adjustment. During the operation of the quota the same price model is apparently assumed to be operative, whereas it may be that the two markets (export and domestic) become decoupled.

A model of price determination

As discussed above, the world coffee market has to be seen as possibly operating in different modes when the quota was effective and when it was not effective. In the quota-off period the world price arbitrages to the producer price, but in the quota-on period these two prices are potentially decoupled. There is a regime change at known points in time (*ex post*). Ideally the imposition of the quotas should itself be modelled as an endogenous variable, linked to the levels of the indicator prices, but this introduces a much more complex modelling problem.

In order to explain the determination of prices a simplified model has been used. The individual equations have already been discussed, so that this section concentrates on the links between endogenous variables, and on the crucial specification of which variables are exogenous.

The key to the modelling of the world price determination is the linking of the supply and demand sides of the model. The statistics provided by the ICO do not give an explicit supply–demand balance so that it is necessary to construct the linking identities.

Producer stocks (of member countries). The total world production (WP) of member states goes to consumption by producing members (PC), to exports to member consuming countries (E), to exports to non-member countries (NMC), and to changes in producer stocks ($DPST$).

$$WP = PC + E + NMC + DPST \tag{1}$$

There are data on all of these categories except for the changes in producer stocks. These are thus derived by using the identity (1). For econometric modelling purposes it is necessary to work with stock *levels*. A value of producer stocks in 1967 is available from the ICO. Using this and the figures calculated for the change in stocks, a series for the level of producer stocks (PST) is calculated.

For the purposes of econometric modelling the exports to non-member countries are taken as exogenous. The consumption of Brazil is modelled explicitly and the consumption of other producing members is taken as exogenous. World production is modelled as in Section 2 above, while exports to consuming members are linked to imports of those countries (see below).

Consumer stocks (of member countries). The total imports (X) into consuming member countries is equal to the disappearance in member countries (MC), plus net re-exports by member countries (R), plus the change in consumer stocks ($DCST$). Data on the first three series are available from the ICO so that the change in consumer stocks is estimated by using the identity:

$$X = MC + R + DCST \qquad (2)$$

Once the change in consumer stocks is known, then the level of consumer stocks is estimated using a known value for 1967 for the level of consumer stocks given by the ICO.

The level of disappearances is modelled as in the demand analysis (Section 1), while re-exports are taken as exogenous.

Supply–demand balance. The exports of producing member countries (E) to consuming members is equal to total imports by the consuming member countries (X) from all sources less the imports of the consuming member countries from non-member producers (N).

$$X = E + N \qquad (3)$$

The figure for N is not published and is estimated by applying the identity (3). This figure inevitably is a 'catch all' and will include errors made elsewhere in the statistics. For the purposes of modelling it is taken as exogenous.

Once these identities are in place it is possible to consider closing the model. The variables still to be modelled are the world price and the stock levels (or changes in stocks) in both the producing countries and consuming countries. If there were a single stock figure it would be natural to follow the cocoa model and relate the price to the world stock-to-consumption ratio. There is then a solution in which the price, for a certain stock level, induces just enough consumption and production that the balance between the two (the change in stocks) when added to the stock level from the previous period is equal to the *level* of stocks assumed to be determining the price. During the period that export quotas were not in operation it is natural to aggregate the identities (1) and (2) to obtain the total change in stock (*DTST*) identity:

$$DTST = DPST + DCST = (WP - PC - NMC - E) \\ + (X - MC - R) \quad (4)$$

Using the initial value for *TST* as calculated from the ICO statistics in 1967 allows *DTST* to be modelled as a single variable with a link to the total stock level.

A price-response equation could then be constructed. The world price (*P*) would be related to the ratio of total stocks to world consumption (*TCON*). World consumption is equal to consumption in member consuming countries plus consumption in member producing countries. This formulation omits consumption by non-member countries, but there are no direct data available on this variable. This approach, in fact, does not allow *X* and *E* to be separately identified as the schematic system of equations shown below indicates:

Core equations:

$$WP = f(P) \qquad (i)$$
$$PC = f(P) \qquad (ii)$$
$$MC = f(P) \qquad (iii)$$
$$DTST = TST - TST(-1) \qquad (iv)$$
$$P = f(TST/[MC + PC]) \qquad (v)$$
$$X - E = N \qquad (vi)$$
$$DTST = WP - PC - NMC - E + X - MC - R \qquad (vii)$$

The variables $TST(-1)$, *N*, *NMC*, and *R* are all exogenous so that there are seven equations but eight endogenous variables: *WP*, *PC*, *MC*, *DTST*, *TST*, *P*, *X*, and *E*. The substitution of (vi) into (vii) solves the identification problem by removing one equation and two variables but the price paid for this is that the exports of producers cannot be modelled. There are various solutions to the problem. If producer stocks were ignored or taken as exogenous (as in the cocoa model), then a figure for exports could be derived. Alternatively a behavioural relation to fix consumer or producer stock changes is required. The volatility of the two derived stock change series suggests that the latter will be needed.

In the period when quotas were in operation the level of exports (E) can be taken as exogenous but the link from the world price to the producer price cannot then be taken to operate as in a quota-off period, so that the nature of the price linking equations is altered.

Putting these arguments together it can be seen that in addition to the model identities three separate sets of price equations are required.

Retail price to world price links

Equations linking retail prices to the world price are needed for all the consuming countries separately identified in the demand section of the model. Equations are estimated for eight large consuming member countries and for Brazil, which as well as being the major producer, is an important consumer.

The model, which is in double log form, relates the nominal retail price to the world coffee price (ICO composite indicator price measured in dollars), the exchange rate against the dollar, and time trend. Experiments in partial adjustment were carried out by introducing lagged values of the exogenous variables and the lagged retail price. For France, Italy, and the UK there was evidence that there is some delay in adjusting to changes in the world coffee price. In several countries the time trend was significant suggesting that the margin for processing and distribution was increasing. Since the data are in nominal prices this was probably a reflection of a general increase in domestic costs.

In every case there is a strong correlation and it is clear that retail prices are closely linked to the world price (see Section A.2.3(a)).

World price to producer price links

For the seven main producing countries (excluding Uganda for lack of data) it is possible to link producer prices (in local currency) to the world price. A double log formulation is used and the exchange rate is introduced to take account of the fact that the world price is measured in dollars.

The intercept of such equations then captures the average mark-up from the producer to the export price on the world market.

Dynamic adjustment is allowed for by introducing lagged dependent or independent variables, but this was generally insignificant, suggesting a rapid arbitrage between markets. A time trend to allow for changes in the mark-up was also tried, but this was significant for only two countries. The resulting equations, reported in Section A.2.3(b), all show a very high degree of fit and the expected signs for all coefficients. Exchange rates and the world price were significant for every country. Only for Côte d'Ivoire is the goodness of fit less good, and this reflects the very strong stance taken by the government in the late 1980s on controlling producer prices.

A crucial test for these equations is to check their stability as between quota-on and quota-off periods. If the quotas were sufficiently restrictive to prevent the world and local prices from arbitraging, then it would be necessary to take explicit account of the level at which the quotas were set. With effective quotas in place, exports from producers to member consumers become exogenous, while producer prices are set so as to clear excess of production over consumption in the producing countries. To test for this regime change a dummy variable for the quota years was introduced (the small sample sizes precluding more elaborate tests)–quotas being used in 1965–71, 1980–4 and 1987–8. In no case was the dummy variable significant. This lends support to the hypothesis that the quotas set actually had little effect on prices, either because they were very little different from what would have been exported in any case, or else because the leakage through non-member countries was sufficiently large to negate their effects. This result allows a single model to be used for the whole period.

The world price and stock level equations

The preceding results are used to justify the continuous operation of a system in which both consumer prices and producer prices arbitrage to the world coffee price.

As pointed out above, it is of considerable interest to be able to identify producer exports, so that it is necessary to have separate equations for consumer stock changes and for producer stock changes. A series of identities (see below) is used to close the formal model. Since the identities in effect can be used to 'fix' one of the stock changes, it is possible to use one stock change equation to give a relation with the world price and then to complete the system by linking the two stock changes together.

The *world price equation* is the focal point of the whole model. In it the log of the world coffee price is related to the log of the ratio of producer stocks to world coffee production, to the lagged world coffee price, a time trend, and a dummy for the quota years (producer stocks were calculated as explained above).

The equation gives a good degree of fit and significant coefficients, (see Section A.2.3(c), equation 1). Experimentation with lags and other possible explanatory variables did not improve the equation. As with the cocoa model, there is a very strong negative relation between the stock/production ratio and the world price.

Neither the time trend nor the quota dummy variable was significant, and both were dropped. The lack of significance of the dummy variable adds weight to the evidence that the operation of the quota system did not make a significant difference to the world price.

The final equation that is needed is one to determine consumer stocks. After a good deal of experimentation, an equation was estimated in which the log of the consumer stock level was related to the log of the world price in the previous period (Section A.2.3(c), equation 2). The goodness of fit was rather disappointing but no other variant was acceptable. Given the potential for errors in the stock data this poor fit is not altogether surprising. The figure for the most recent year in the calculations (1990) is particularly suspect, showing a near 40 per cent increase in consumer stocks over 1989 at a time when disappearances in consumer countries also grew strongly. No model could be found to give an acceptable fit to the 1990 figure.

The closing identities

To close the model a series of identities are required as shown in Section A.2.3(c). The consumption identities add together all the explicitly modelled consumption with the consumption of members from the rest of the world (*RWCONS*), which itself is made up consumption (disappearance) from other member consumers and consumption from other member producers. Two other identities aggregate to consumption (disappearance) of all member consumers (*MC*) and consumption of all member producers (*PC*).

The supply identity aggregates the production of all modelled countries with that of the rest of member producers to give total member production (*WP*).

The stock identities begin with those outlined in the text for changes in member producer stocks, for changes in member consumer stocks and for stock changes related to stock levels. The stock/consumption and stock/production variables are defined by two further identities, and finally, closing the model, exports from member countries to member countries are related to imports into member countries from all sources.

The system of equations as a whole contains forty behavioural equations and twelve identities.

9

The World Tea Market

9.1 THE DEMAND FOR TEA

There have been some gradual changes over the post-war period in the form in which tea is consumed, with instant tea becoming more important in certain markets. This has had the effect that the quantity of tea required to produce a given quantity of the beverage has declined. Akiyama and Trivedi (1987) cite a study by Goradia which estimated that during the period 1951 to 1970 the global consumption of liquid tea rose by 145 per cent, while the consumption of tea-leaves rose by only 92 per cent. Such a figure may be somewhat exaggerated once the enormous size of the markets in China and the USSR is included, but nevertheless it may be expected that there is some downward trend due to this factor.

The principal determinants of tea consumption, as with coffee, can be expected to be real income, the real retail price of tea, and the price of tea relative to its close substitutes. In addition, population size will have an important effect, particularly in the large consuming countries of Asia. The functional form of the per capita demand equations might be expected to show the effects of saturation at high levels of tea consumption.

Previous studies

There have been relatively few published econometric studies of the world tea market so that there is only limited evidence on the size of the price and income elasticities. The study by Chung and Ukpong (1981) describes some unpublished studies by FAO and UNCTAD, but does not report in detail on the models or their findings. The later study by Akiyama and Trivedi reviews the published work on tea; but all of these predate the Chung and Upkong study and hence are now considerably out of date.

Both of these studies estimate demand equations for several countries using the import data (apparent consumption). The earlier study used a double log (constant elasticity formulation) to link per capita consumption to per capita real GDP and the price of tea relative to the price of coffee (both measured in US cents/lb). The price series used were the 'world' prices for tea and coffee rather than the local retail prices because of lack of data for the appropriate price series. Time trends were also included to capture changing tastes and changing technology.

Chung and Ukpong's results show an almost uniformly low price elasticity of demand (one-half of the countries covered having elasticities of -0.02 or less), coupled with substantial income elasticities in the majority of cases. The UK is, however, a major exception with a negative income elasticity (-0.80), indicating a very strong shift away from tea consumption. In addition, negative time trends were identified for all the industrialized countries. A negative income elasticity is shown also for Indonesia, which can be attributed in part to the limited availability of domestic green tea, and in part to the errors induced by using the apparent consumption figures. It is also possible that the relative price variable was not appropriate for certain countries where coffee is not a popular beverage. The real price of tea is also a variable that should have been included in case the substitution against all other goods was important.

The study by Akiyama and Trivedi relates per capita consumption (disappearance) to the retail tea price in real terms measured in local currency, the real price of substitutes (coffee), real GDP, and a time trend. The functional form used was mainly semi-logarithmic in order to yield declining price and income elasticities. For some countries there were no data available on retail prices, so the world tea price converted into local currency was used as the proxy for retail prices. The period of estimation varied in its starting-date but generally covered the period from the mid-1960s to 1984. For many countries, the income variable was insignificant.

The results of this study confirm the low price elasticities found in the earlier study, with one-half of the countries having elasticities of −0.20 or less. For the estimated income elasticities, however, there was a significant negative coefficient for India, while for a majority of countries the computed income elasticity was not statistically significant. None the less, for the Middle East countries included, the elasticities were significant and substantial (ranging from 0.76 for Syria to 0.98 for Egypt), indicating major change in the pattern of world demand for tea. The difference between the two studies cannot be attributed to the inclusion of time trends since both studies incorporated them. The different periods covered and the very different price variables are likely to be the most important factors in explaining the difference in results. For a few countries, the price of substitutes (coffee) or complements (sugar) was found to be significant.

The coverage of the latter study is less well focused on the important consumers. It omits China, Japan, and Iran, while including some relatively small consumers. Both studies omit Turkey (the world's fifth largest consumer) and Iraq. Since Turkey trades so little tea its omission may be relatively unimportant as regards the world scene.

A key point emphasized by both studies is the period of declining demand in certain countries—notably the UK. Standard demand models inevitably have produced negative income elasticities to explain this fact. For the purposes of extrapolation this is very important because it produces a steady fall in demand from the fourth largest consuming country. The addition of more recent data than that used in the most up-to-date study available (finishing in 1984) may be able to shed some light on developments in the UK market.

The present study

The aim of the demand section of the present study is to concentrate on the major consumers of tea. Lack of economic data on the former Soviet Union makes it impossible to estimate an equation for that country, so that its consumption is taken to be exogenous for the purposes of the policy simulations. There are data available for eleven other major consumers, including some producing countries (China, India, Turkey, Indonesia, and Kenya) and some importing countries (UK, USA, Iran, Pakistan, Japan, and Egypt).

The measurement of demand itself is an approximation for both sets of countries, since there are no published data on demand. For producers, demand is estimated as production less exports (plus any imports). Changes in stocks will thus be included in demand—but since tea cannot be stored for long the incremental stocks are unlikely to be important with respect to the level of demand. For the non-producing countries, net imports (disappearances) are used and again retail stocks are unknown, except for the UK, where net imports are adjusted for stock changes.

A substantial problem for all tea studies has been the lack of retail price data. The ITC does not publish such data and there is little available on a lengthy time-series basis from elsewhere. For India, UK, and the USA retail prices were available, but for other countries a proxy was constructed using a series for the world price of tea (in $) converted by the exchange rate and deflated by the local cost of living index. The form of the demand equations was one in which the per capita consumption of tea was related to per capita real income and the real price of tea in the local market. Lags on both explanatory variables were tried, and the equations were estimated in both linear and log-linear form.

For two countries it proved difficult to fit an income term. In the UK, the steady fall in overall consumption throughout the period from the early 1960s to 1991 meant that income elasticities were inevitably negative. It is quite possible that, in the case of the UK, tea has been an inferior good—probably the number of cups of tea has not declined so strongly, but the amount of tea used per cup has certainly fallen. The best equation in fact omitted income and included a (negative) trend. The USA has very cyclical data on disappearances (probably related to inventory movements) but there appears to be a trend with some saturation level. Various experiments on non-linear functions were tried, but in no case could any income variable be identified. Further detailed work on these two important markets is called for.

Table 9.1 *Estimated price and income elasticities of demand for tea*

	Price	Income		Price	Income
UK	−0.17	—	Japan	−0.09	0.64
US	−0.47	—	Pakistan	—	0.80
China	—	0.70	Turkey	—	2.93
India	—	0.84	Egypt	−0.16	1.24
Indonesia	−0.66	1.12	Kenya	−0.88	3.75
Iran	−0.23	0.24	Rest of world	—	0.53

Source: Section A.3.1

The equations for other countries behaved more as expected, although it was necessary to start some equations in the 1970s (e.g. for Egypt, to allow for the switch to a liberalized import policy). The results for the elasticities are shown in Table 9.1 and the equations are given in Section A.3.1. These results are very striking. All the countries covered, apart from the mature markets of the UK and the USA, have strong income elasticities, while in general price elasticities are fairly small. For the important markets of China, India, Pakistan, and Turkey, it was not possible to identify a significant (negative) price effect on demand. These results suggest that the market for tea will continue to grow as the income and population of the major consuming countries continue to increase.

9.2 THE SUPPLY OF TEA

Tea shares the principal characteristics of the supply of cocoa and coffee in that it is a tree crop which does not yield immediately on planting and which has a long life. The total output thus depends not only on the total acreage planted, but also on the age structure of the tree stock. Tea starts to yield around its fifth year and the yields increase to a peak around ten years of age. Thereafter, there is only a very slow decline until an advanced age (sixty or more years) is reached. For countries where the crop is well established and the annual change in acreage is relatively small, the yield would be correspondingly little affected by changes in the age structure. However, for relatively new producers, where the incremental area is substantial in relation to total area, yields can be expected to vary.

If the yield profile over the life of a bush is the same, irrespective of when it was planted (no technical progress), the life is very long with respect to the age at which peak yield is reached, and if there is a constant growth rate in acreage, then yields will rise, but in a non-linear fashion. With infinite lives, the upper asymptote for average yield is the maximum yield for an individual bush. Since tea bushes have a very long life (60–100 years), those countries with a long history of production would not be expected to show a substantial trend in yields due to the pure age-composition effect. Newer producers, particularly Kenya among the larger countries, might be expected to show an increase in average productivity of a non-linear form.

In addition, however, there has been technical progress in terms of varieties of bush planted. Yields have thus been driven up and, in effect, the upper asymptote for the average yield has increased. Detailed agronomic studies could indicate how important this effect has been. Clearly a trend in past yields cannot be extrapolated as if the trend in the asymptotic average yield will increase constantly with time. If marginal land is less productive than trend, yields can fall. For an *ex post* simulation model it is merely necessary to distinguish these effects from those of prices, so that policy responses can be evaluated under the assumption that the policy being investigated would not have changed the yield pattern.

In addition to this age effect and technological (vintage) effect on output, there are two other sets of factors to consider. Firstly, there is the actual area of bearing bushes and, secondly, there are the short-run determinants of yields.

The area harvested depends on previous planting decisions, as well as on uprooting decisions. Under the assumption that all bushes come into production at a given age (around five or six years in practice), then the area harvested in year t can be given by the recurrence relation

$$H_t = H_{t-1} + N_{t-6} - U_t, \tag{1}$$

where H = area harvested; N = new planted area; and U = uprooted area. For certain countries, notably India and Sri Lanka, there are data on these various components, so that a fully articulated area equation could be built up from the separate decisions. Tea production is very much a multi-input sector, requiring a large degree of labour for harvesting plus infrastructure for the workforce. The need to sink such costs implies that exit and entry of acreage does not occur easily. The key factors for new acreage are the price of tea and the price of labour (relative to other local costs both of inputs and competing outputs).

The yield of tea varies not only because of the age of the bush and because of its vintage, but it can also vary to some extent because of economic decisions as to how extensively to pluck the bush. So called 'coarse plucking' can increase the quantity but at the expense of current quality and future quantity. High prices may thus lead to temporary increases in yield. Although the weather is important in determining yield, for given locations it is unusual to have large enough climatic variations to produce substantial shifts in output (unlike the effect of frosts on Brazilian coffee output).

Previous studies

The two major studies for supply modelling are those already described in Section 1. The earlier study by Chung and Ukpong constructs separate equations for the yield and for mature (yielding) area. Following equation (1) the mature area (defined as the total area planted six years previously) is regressed on its own value lagged one period, on the seven-year lagged price of tea (at London) deflated by a cost index and a time trend. A double log specification was used and the data were for the period 1957–78. In virtually all cases the coefficient of the price term was insignificant. This may be in part due to the measurement of prices. The tea price (world price) was either deflated by the world coffee price (for African and Latin American producers), or by a fertilizer price (US price of ammonium sulphate). Both formulations take the world tea price as equivalent to the tea price received by producers, and also implicitly assume that alterations in the exchange rate will have no effect on producers' decisions. In this approach no local costs enter the equations. The non-linear formulation is also a problem since equation (1) postulates a linear relation, with the coefficient on lagged acreage equal to unity.

To this area equation, a yield equation (output divided by mature area) was added. Yield was regressed on the real tea price lagged one and ten periods (but not on the current price) and on a trend. Again, a double log specification was used for data covering 1957–78. Only for India, Indonesia, and Uganda were significant price elasticities found. The separate equations were also replaced by a single output equation (related to area and prices lagged one and seven periods), but again there was little evidence of any supply response to changing prices. The countries included six individual countries and six groups so that the study covered all world production.

The later study by Akiyama and Trivedi used a variety of equations depending on data availability for each country. Equations for new plantings, uprootings, and replantings were estimated for India and Sri Lanka, while for Kenya and Malawi there was an equation for net change in planted area. In all cases new plantings show some responsiveness to prices. The price was measured as the local auction price deflated by a cost of living index.

The output equation is either built up using a full vintage model or some approximation to it dependent on data

Table 9.2 *Short-run price elasticities of supply of tea*

	Current year	1 year lag
India	0.13	0.15
Sri Lanka	0.03	—
Kenya:		
Smallholders	0.17	0.23
Estates	0.25	0.52
Malawi	0.21	0.18
Indonesia	—	0.16
Bangladesh	0.17	—
Rest of Africa	—	0.11
China	0.15	—

Source: Akiyama and Trivedi (1982)

availability. Short-run price elasticities, which show the responsiveness of yield to price, are reported in Table 9.2.

This table indicates that yields were responsive to price changes. The difference from the earlier study may well be due to the more appropriate measure of producer prices used. No direct estimates for long-run elasticities were given, but simulations of policy changes indicate that after a five-to-six-year period, the effect of higher prices on acreage and hence on output could also be detected.

The present study

The two approaches to modelling the supply of tea were considered, i.e. a yield approach and a production approach. In both cases it was decided to treat area as exogenous, even though in the long run it can be expected to respond to prices. Because the simulations of alternative policies for tea discussed in Chapter 5 cover only a six-year period, the long lag between prices and area harvested means that the policy shifts are not expected to affect area within the period considered.

The output equations would relate output to area harvested, to a measure of producer prices and to a time trend to catch long-run productivity effects. The yield equations relate yield to prices, to area, and to time trends. Output is then derived by multiplying the endogenous yield by the exogenous area.

The data for these equations have some important shortcomings. In no case is there a time-series available for producer prices of tea, so that a proxy has to be found. A preliminary exercise correlated the 'world price of tea' (London auction) converted into local currency with the local auction price, where available. In most cases, this correlation was very high and it was decided that the simplest approach would be to use the converted world price. For India, however, the prices were substantially different so that the local auction price is used as a producer price. Where no local auction price existed (e.g. for China) then the world price expressed in local currency was used.

For Sri Lanka the data on area harvested appeared unreliable (at one point registering no change for several years), so that it is not surprising that no model was successful, and Sri Lanka had to be omitted. Since it is an important exporter its exports were aggregated into the 'rest of the world' equation, which is discussed below.

Models were constructed for seven individual producers—the Soviet Union also being excluded because of lack of data—both output and yield equations being tried for all countries. In the output equations, the level of output was related to the area harvested, to the local price of tea in real terms, to a trend term, and to lagged variables. Area was always significant, while the real tea price was only significant for Turkey, Japan, and China. Positive trends were found for Iran and Indonesia. The goodness of fit was generally reasonable, with a poorer fit for China, but for Kenya and China the Durbin–Watson statistic was very low, suggesting misspecification.

The yield equations were generally more satisfactory. The yield was regressed (in a linear model) on area harvested, on real prices, and a time trend. Experiments with lags on prices were carried out. The preferred equations are shown in Section A.3.2.

For three of the four major exporters (India, China, and Kenya) there was evidence of sensitivity to real prices (in local currency)—while for Indonesia no evidence of price sensitivity could be identified. For all countries except Japan and Iran, there was a positive time trend, but for most countries the area harvested had a negative coefficient. These two factors suggest a combination of decreasing returns to area coupled with increasing productivity due to improved varieties, etc. For the major producers, the goodness of fit was high and the Durbin–Watson statistic did not indicate severe misspecification. Only for Japan and Iran were the results less satisfactory; however, these countries are of more limited importance in world trade in tea. The price elasticities of supply derived from the yield equations range from 0.16 for India, to 0.26 for China, 0.28 for Turkey, and 0.30 for Kenya. Coupled with the price elasticities of demand presented in Section 1, the evidence is that the trade in tea is sensitive to prices.

Finally, a 'rest of the world equation' was estimated. In order that this should close the model it was decided to relate the exports of tea of all other producers to the area harvested in these countries, to a time trend and to the world price in US dollars (since no exchange rate could be identified for this heterogeneous group). The price term was insignificant, so that for the policy simulations this variable is effectively exogenous.

9.3   THE DETERMINATION OF TEA PRICES

The model, as described in preceding sections, uses three levels of tea prices, viz. prices paid by consumers, prices received by producers and the world tea price. These various prices are linked together by a series of equations and the world price is taken as being market-clearing.

Retail prices

The lack of data on tea prices meant that genuine retail prices were available only for India, the UK, and the USA. For all other countries a proxy was constructed by taking the world price and deflating by the exchange rate. These latter price links then enter the model as a series of identities. For the three countries where separate series existed, behavioural equations were estimated linking the local retail price to the world price expressed in local currency (see Section A.3.4(a)). For the USA, lagged retail prices were significant, indicating that there is partial adjustment in that country to changes in the world price.

Producer price

In the case of all producers, except India, there were no data available on producer prices, and local auction prices were very similar to the world tea price (expressed in local currency). Thus, for these countries the price link is again given by the identity converting the world price into a local currency price. For India, an equation was estimated which related the local price to the exchange rate, the world price, and a time trend to allow for changing differentials and domestic margins. (Section A.3.4(b)).

The world price

The key price in the world tea model is the world market price, which was taken to be the London tea auction price. Although London does not now have the central importance it once had for the physical trading of tea, it is still highly visible and there appears to be strong arbitrage between the different international tea prices (see Friedheim (1992)).

Since stocks are of much less importance for tea than for coffee or cocoa (due to their perishability), they function more as pipeline stocks rather than as a means of regulating the market or responding to expectations of year-to-year price or quantity shifts.

The world tea price (in $) is related to the ratio of UK tea stocks to world exports, and to its own lagged value to allow for partial adjustment. This equation fits moderately well but the price 'spikes' of 1977 and 1984, noted in Chapter 2, are not well explained. Accordingly, these years are given separate dummy variables. Experiments with the lagged stock/export ratio and with general consumer prices did not lead to any improvement. The final equation indicates a significant negative effect for the stock/export ratio as well as a significant degree of partial adjustment of prices to changes in this ratio. (Section A.3.4(c)).

With so much of the world's tea production being consumed in the producing countries, it was decided to relate the exports of the producers to the imports of the non-producers (plus imports by producers whose output was less than domestic consumption). Hence, from the models of Sections 9.1 and 9.2 above, a series of identities linking exports to production less consumption were constructed for India, China, Kenya, Indonesia, Iran, Japan, and Turkey (allowing for imports where necessary). To these were added the exports of the 'rest of the world' sector to give total exports (which are a function of world prices).

World imports are the disappearances of tea in the separately identified countries (USA, UK, Pakistan, Egypt) plus the rest of the world, where the latter has been measured as world imports less those of the four countries mentioned, and the small amount of imports into Japan and Iran. In the data of the ITC world exports and imports are not exactly equal, and a small balancing item defines their difference—this is taken as exogenous in the policy simulations. Hence, the equality between exports and imports in effect determines the world price.

For the UK there are data on wholesale stocks so that imports can be split into net stock changes plus disappearances (consumption plus changes in retail stocks). Section 9.1 used disappearances for UK demand, so that a separate stock identity is needed to complete the determination of world imports.

ANNEXE

A Model of Import Shares

A detailed picture of the main flows of international trade in tea is given for a recent year (1991) in Table 9.3. Certain countries are, however, omitted. Turkey, for example, a major tea producer and consumer, had relatively little foreign trade in tea; Iraq, also a major tea consumer in the 1980s, imported little in 1991. By contrast, Germany and the Netherlands, though relatively unimportant consumers, did import substantial amounts which were then re-exported.

The most important import markets for tea in 1991 were the UK, the former Soviet Union, Pakistan, the USA, Iran, and Egypt. The former Soviet Union relied very heavily on imports from India, with a substantial share coming from China, but for all other import markets there was a much lower concentration of sources. It is particularly notable that the three developing countries in this list all imported from a wide range of sources rather than tying themselves to a narrow range of suppliers. Many factors are likely to determine the patterns of this country-to-country trade and its variation over time, but the role of relative prices is of central importance because the impact of economic policies designed to affect the tea market will work through the general level of tea prices and through the relative prices of competing exports. The remainder of this Annexe investigates the sensitivity of trade shares of rival suppliers to their relative prices in each of the major markets.

There has been very little analysis of individual country-to-country trade flows for primary commodities and apparently no published study of the world tea market. A recent detailed study by Lord (1991) concentrated on Latin American producers, for whom tea is generally an unimportant commodity. However the approach used by Lord provides a good starting-point for the analysis of tea. In this model the imports of tea are hypothesized to be determined according to a two-stage budgeting process. The country first determines its total

Table 9.3 *Trade flows of tea exports, 1991 ('000 tonnes)*

	India	Sri Lanka	Indonesia	China	Kenya	Malawi	Tanzania	Bangladesh	Argentina	Rest of world	Total
UK	22.6	11.7	6.9	6.3	72.5	25.4	5.3		1.6	29.0	181.3
Germany	4.7	3.6	3.4	2.2	1.4	1.0	0.4	0.4	2.6	5.6	25.3
Netherlands	1.9	2.8	6.0	1.8	6.0	4.6	0.2	0.3	2.9	2.8	29.3
USSR	104.5	5.1	12.5	35.4				2.0		8.5	168.0
Canada	0.6	2.2	0.6	0.8	2.2				0.1	7.0	13.5
USA	2.6	3.3	13.1	21.4	3.7		0.3		16.5	25.2	85.8
Iran	14.8	31.7	4.5	0.7	2.3					10.6	75.0
Pakistan	0.3	7.8	22.3	2.4	44.8	4.2	8.9	10.4	0.5	16.7	113.2
Egypt	7.9	20.4	15.7	0.3	21.0			5.3		1.3	70.2
Morocco	1.5			28.4				3.6		−5.2	24.7
Australia	0.7	2.9	5.2	2.8	0.9				0.1	4.7	17.3
Japan	2.0	5.3	0.4	15.6	0.4					13.4	37.1
Other	38.8	114.0	19.6	66.8	20.4	6.0	1.8	3.4	11.7	−42.2	240.8
Total	202.9	210.8	110.2	184.9	175.6	41.2	17.5	25.4	36.0	77	1,081.5

Source: Annual Bulletin of Statistics (various issues), International Tea Committee, London.

tea imports with reference to an average price of tea, the prices of other commodities, real income, etc. At the second stage, the shares in the total volume of imports are determined by the relative prices of the different sources of tea imports. Putting these two stages together generates country-by-country trade flows.

The focal point of the present analysis is to model the shares equations so that cross-price elasticities of demand between different sources of supply can be estimated. The model used by Lord for this aspect is particularly simple:

$$W_i = \alpha_i (P_i/P)^\gamma, \tag{1}$$

where W_i is the volume share of imports from source i into the country in question; P_i is the price of imports from source i; P is the general price of all (tea) imports; and α_i, γ are parameters to be estimated. This formulation does not, however, allow for specific pairwise cross-price effects. All rival prices work only through the general price index.

A more general approach, widely used in modelling demands for factor inputs (see Berndt (1991) for a full account) is to start with a translog utility function. From this the expenditure shares of imports from individual sources in the total import bill for tea can be derived as:

$$V_i = \alpha_i + \sum_j \alpha_{ij} \ln P_j \tag{2}$$

for each i. The summation is over all prices (including the own price). In order to ensure that the share equations sum to unity and that they are consistent with an underlying utility maximization, certain parameter restrictions must be imposed:

$$\sum_i \alpha_i = 1 \tag{3}$$

$$\sum_j \alpha_{ij} = 0 \text{ all i} \tag{4}$$

$$\alpha_{ij} = \alpha_{ji} \text{ all i,j} \tag{5}$$

For example, in a three-source model, the expenditure shares into a given country become:

$$V_1 = \alpha_1 + \alpha_{11}(\ln P_1 - \ln P_3) + \alpha_{12}(\ln P_2 - \ln P_3) \tag{6}$$

$$V_2 = \alpha_2 + \alpha_{12}(\ln P_1 - \ln P_3) + \alpha_{22}(\ln P_2 - \ln P_3) \tag{7}$$

The third equation is completely determined by the parameters of the first two coupled with the restrictions, and hence estimation of only two equations would be required. This must be done by a 'system' method which imposes the common parameter restriction.

From such a system the partial-own and cross-price elasticities and Hicks–Allen elasticities of substitution can be estimated. They are given by the formulae:

$$e_{ij} = (\alpha_{ij} + S_i S_j)/S_i \tag{8}$$

$$e_{ii} = (\alpha_{ii} + S_i^2 - S_i)/S_i \tag{9}$$

and

$$\sigma_{ij} = e_{ij}/S_j \tag{10}$$

$$\sigma_{ii} = e_{ii}/S_i \tag{11}$$

where the S_i are the (mean) share values at which the elasticities are to be evaluated. The interpretation of these elasticities is that both individual prices and the total demand for imports are held constant. One price is then changed and the percentage change in the quantities purchased is related to the percentage change in this price, while just enough substitution between teas takes place to hold the total import volume constant.

The data on trade flows presented earlier reveal that four market economies buy tea in substantial amounts from several sources—the UK, the USA, Egypt, and Pakistan. There are, however, no disaggregated trade flow data specified by value and volume for imports into Egypt, so that the present analysis concentrates on the other three cases. The (gross) import data have the benefit of identifying all the flows into a country at a given time so that it is not necessary to estimate total imports and the residual from non-specified sources by a scaling factor.

The identification of imports from separate countries as being distinct items in the two-stage utility function implies that all teas from a given producer are fairly homogeneous, but that teas from different countries are distinct. The strengths of the relative preferences for these various imports will interact with their relative prices to determine import shares. The country-to-country trade flow data show both value and quantity so that import unit values can be calculated. These unit value indices are assumed to reflect retail prices, and this will be an adequate measure for relative shares provided all teas have the same percentage mark-up in a given year (though the common mark-up could change from year to year).

The UK buys from the widest range of suppliers—over the period 1974–91 (the longest for which data were available when the analysis was made), there were seven major suppliers (Zimbabwe exported tea to the UK only from 1980). The residual category accounted for a mean share of 14 per cent of the total value of imports during the period. Experiments using the basic expenditure shares model (with restrictions) showed, firstly, that there was a considerable gain in efficiency in using Zellner's Seemingly Unrelated Regressions estimator (SUR) rather than equation-by-equation ordinary least squares. Secondly, it was found that adding a time trend improved the results further—the coefficient on the trend in the last equation would be equal to the sum of all the other trend coefficients, and opposite in sign in order to preserve the additive properties of the share equations. Each of the seven estimated equations thus includes nine regression coefficients compared to the eighteen years data. Rather than present the detailed regressions Table 9.4 gives the estimated partial price elasticities and some summary statistics for each equation. The column labels represent the quantity being determined while the rows correspond to the various determining prices.

The first feature of the table to note is that not only are all the own price elasticities negative, but that for most sources of tea they are substantial. The second important feature is that in every case, bar that of Malawi, Kenyan tea is a strong substitute. Even after removing trends in the shares of each tea in the UK market, shares of all teas fell as the price of Kenyan tea fell. Some teas appeared to be complementary—

Table 9.4 *Own and cross-price elasticities for teas imported into the UK 1974–1991*

	India Share	Sri Lanka Share	Indonesia Share	China Share	Kenya Share	Malawi Share	Tanzania Share	Other Share
India Price	-0.434	0.746	-2.267	-1.704	0.475	-0.109	0.626	0.242
Sri Lanka Price	0.269	-1.265	-1.546	1.718	0.339	-0.237	-1.213	0.045
Indonesia Price	-0.306	-0.577	-3.552	1.267	0.307	0.487	1.740	0.122
China Price	-0.242	0.676	1.334	-1.340	0.176	-0.423	-0.538	0.078
Kenya Price	0.527	1.043	2.526	1.373	-1.453	-0.169	1.030	0.118
Malawi Price	-0.038	-0.225	1.239	-1.025	-0.052	-0.292	1.629	0.028
Tanzania Price	0.090	-0.481	1.847	-0.542	0.133	0.679	-3.176	-0.043
Other Price	0.134	0.083	0.419	0.266	0.076	0.065	-0.010	-0.619
Mean Share	0.265	0.096	0.036	0.038	0.294	0.091	0.038	0.144
SEE	0.035	0.010	0.009	0.006	0.024	0.015	0.008	0.014
Trend Coefficient	-0.014	-0.007	0.003	0.002	0.017	0.004	-0.001	-0.004
R^2	0.77	0.89	0.22	0.79	0.96	0.63	0.58	0.87
DWS	1.79	2.20	2.62	2.67	1.93	1.74	2.02	1.22

this may be because they were seen as equivalent by the consumer, e.g. if Kenyan prices fall leading to a rise in the consumption of Kenyan tea, some consumers may be willing to buy more Malawian tea on the grounds that it is also African and its desirability has increased. The blending of teas together will also affect these cross-price effects. The goodness of fit of the equations is generally very good and a large number of the individual regression coefficients were statistically significant, apart from the intercept and trend. Exact significance tests on the price elasticities are not available since they are non-linear functions of the regression parameters.

The next country to be analysed is the USA. Here the volume of tea imported has been cyclical but has not shown the long-term decline of the UK. There have been four major sources of imports, with Sri Lanka steadily declining in importance while Argentina and China have both grown very strongly. The results for the price elasticities are shown in Table 9.5.

The results for the USA are less good than for those for the UK. The residual sector, made up of several small imports, is much larger than for the UK and tends to dominate the results. The own-price elasticities are of the incorrect sign for Indonesian and Argentinian imports. It appears that price competition between teas has not been a central feature in determining the shares of imports into the US market.

Table 9.5 *Own and cross-price elasticities for teas imported into the US 1974–1991*

	Sri Lanka share	Indonesia share	China share	Argentina share	Other share
Sri Lanka price	−1.200	−0.196	0.386	0.154	0.319
Indonesia price	−0.197	0.362	−0.039	0.938	−0.189
China price	0.249	−0.025	−1.200	0.187	0.135
Argentina price	0.080	0.490	0.150	0.293	−0.246
Other price	1.066	−0.633	0.700	−1.580	−0.020
Mean share	0.154	0.153	0.099	0.080	0.513
SEE	0.009	0.012	0.009	0.011	0.015
Trend coefficient	−0.015	0.007	0.009	0.013	−0.014
R^2	0.981	0.720	0.973	0.911	0.701
DWS	2.23	2.49	1.29	1.73	1.93

The third set of results relates to Pakistan, which has stead-ily increased the volume of its imports during the period. There are four major sources of imports (Sri Lanka, Indonesia, Kenya, and Bangladesh) and the residual sector, with a mean share of 19 per cent, is not dominant as in the USA. The results are shown in Table 9.6 and are generally less satisfact-ory. Only the 'other tea' category has a negative own-price coefficient and there is little pattern to the cross-price elasti-cities. The goodness of fit is considerably worse than for the UK or the USA. Detailed examination of the shares data reveals very substantial year-to-year variations that are likely to be due to factors other than changes in relative prices.

Putting these results together, for three important import-ers of tea that have purchased from several sources, suggests that where markets are well established, as in the UK, an important factor in explaining year-to-year changes in the source of imports is the relative prices of competing teas. Even in this case there are trends in shares, not associated with price differentials. Such trends may be related to advert-ising and learning about new sources of supply.

In markets where tea is less important, as in the USA, or is rapidly growing in importance, as in Pakistan, other factors appear to dominate the determination of market shares. For modelling, this suggests that the pure utility based approach may need to be supplemented by a more *ad hoc* modelling which allows for the introduction of situation-specific factors.

Table 9.6 *Own and cross-price elasticities for teas imported into Pakistan (1974–1991)*

	Sri Lanka share	Indonesia share	Kenya share	Bangladesh share	Other share
Sri Lanka price	1.266	−3.816	0.058	−1.230	2.119
Indonesia price	−2.418	2.535	−1.119	3.424	0.717
Kenya price	0.079	−2.405	1.993	−1.936	−0.345
Bangladesh price	−0.631	2.779	−0.729	0.875	−0.730
Other price	1.699	0.907	−0.203	−1.141	−1.760
Mean share	0.232	0.147	0.316	0.119	0.186
SEE	0.049	0.028	0.068	0.053	0.040
Trend coefficient	−0.036	0.012	0.010	0.004	0.010
R^2	0.916	0.429	0.765	0.428	0.701
DWS	2.20	1.36	2.11	1.63	1.55

Such an approach inevitably requires a more detailed knowledge of the markets involved and would be difficult to integrate into a world tea model in which country-by-country trade flows were determined in addition to total imports and exports.

Statistical Appendix

Statistical Appendix

A Estimated Equations for the Econometric Models

A.1 The Cocoa Model

A.1.1 The demand for cocoa

1. USA (1962–90)
$$DPC = -0.383 + 0.219\,YPC - 0.0093\,RCP(-1)$$
$$\quad (0.860) \quad (5.278) \qquad (9.262)$$
$$-0.014\,RSP - 0.046\,TIME$$
$$\quad (2.465) \qquad (4.280)$$

$R^2 = 0.873$, $DW = 2.19$, $Mean = 1.78$, $SEE = 0.087$

2. UK (1961–90)
$$DPC = 0.697 + 0.061\,YPC - 0.0129\,RCP(-1)$$
$$\quad (3.023) \quad (2.273) \qquad (5.096)$$
$$+0.643\,DPC(-1)$$
$$\quad (6711)$$

$R^2 = 0.841$, $Mean = 2.137$, $SEE = 0.133$

3. West Germany (1961–89)
$$DPC = 1.088 + 0.012\,YPC - 0.0028\,RCP$$
$$\quad (3.377) \quad (1.902) \qquad (2.721)$$
$$+0.556\,DPC(-1)$$
$$\quad (4.092)$$

$R^2 = 0.663$, $Mean = 2.650$, $SEE = 0.142$

4. France (1961–90)
$$DPC = 0.582 + 0.019\,YPC - 0.00088\,RCP(-1)$$
$$\quad (8.290)(20.216) \qquad (5.318)$$

$R^2 = 0.938$, $DW = 2.040$, $Mean = 1.789$, $SEE = 0.082$

5. Japan (1961–90)
$DPC = 0.379 + (6.44 \times 10^{-5})\, YPC - (7.94 \times 10^{-6})\, RCP$
   (6.528)   (3.248)   (2.299)
   $-(1.55 \times 10^{-5})\, RCP(-1) + 0.396\, DPC(-1)$
   (3.725)   (3.744)

$R^2 = 0.927, \quad Mean = 0.536, \quad SEE = 0.047$

6. Spain (1962–90)
$DPC = 0.802 + 0.0016\, YPC - (7.419 \times 10^{-5})\, RCP$
   (3.51)   (2.46)   (5.83)
   $-(6.987 \times 10^{-5})\, RCP(-2) - 0.023\, TIME$
   (5.61)   (2.045)

$R^2 = 0.77, \quad DW = 1.40, \quad Mean = 0.859, \quad SEE = 0.116$

7. Belgium (1960–89)
$DPC = 1.324 + 0.0044\, YPC - 0.00023\, RCP$
   (5.10)   (7.29)   (1.96)

$R^2 = 0.66, \quad DW = 1.63, \quad Mean = 2.79, \quad SEE = 0.306$

8. Switzerland (1960–90)
$DPC = 1.586 + 0.0818\, YPC - 0.0054\, RCP$
   (4.36)   (7.94)   (3.15)

$R^2 = 0.77, \quad DW = 1.75, \quad Mean = 3.78, \quad SEE = 0.250$

9. Canada (1961–89)
$DPC = 1.934 + 0.010\, YPC - 0.011\, RPP(-1)$
   (14.53)   (1.09)   (6.19)

$R^2 = 0.61, \quad DW = 1.33, \quad Mean = 1.72, \quad SEE = 0.252$

10. Rest of the World (1976–89)

   Total cocoa consumption $= -62.1 + 4.334 \times$ Developing coun-
                          (0.9) (7.05)   tries Real *GDP*
                          -0.188 Real \$ price of cocoa (-1)
                          (0.90)

   $R^2 = 0.913, \quad DW = 2.12, \quad Mean = 337, \quad SEE = 18.1$

Key
DPC = consumption of cocoa ('000 tonnes) per capita
(million).
YPC = real GNP per capita in 1985 prices.
RCP = real cocoa price (Ghana spot price in London times
exchange rate divided by consumer price index).
RSP = real sugar price (raw sugar price in London times
exchange rate divided by consumer price index).
TIME = time trend.

A.1.2   The Production of Cocoa

A.1.2(a)   Output Equations
1. Ghana (1967–90)

$$O = -100.8 + 0.221\,A + 0.234\,RP(-1)$$
$$\quad\quad (1.50)(3.43) \quad\quad (3.81)$$

$$R^2 = 0.74, \quad DW = 1.43, \quad Mean = 305, \quad SEE = 48.7$$

2. Nigeria (1967–90)

$$O = 62.3 + 0.272A + 1.016\,RP(-1) - 7.78\,TIME$$
$$\quad (0.5)\ (1.59)\quad (2.99)\quad\quad\quad (8.14)$$

$$R^2 = 0.78, \quad DW = 1.98, \quad Mean = 187, \quad SEE = 25.9$$

3. Indonesia (1965–90)

$$O = -11.0 + 0.859\,A + 0.731\,TIME$$
$$\quad\quad (2.9)\ (8.21)\quad (1.93)$$

$$R^2 = 0.90, \quad DW = 1.66, \quad Mean = 19.3, \quad SEE = 9.8$$

4. Malaysia (1969–90)

$$O = -76.3 + 0.772\,A + 1.74\,RP(-2)$$
$$\quad\quad (2.3)(10.63)\quad (2.06)$$

$$R^2 = 0.90, \quad DW = 1.14, \quad Mean = 68.6, \quad SEE = 26.4$$

5. Cameroon (1966–90)

$$O = 33.1 + 0.191\,A(-1)$$
$$\quad (1.1)\ (2.60)$$

$$R^2 = 0.23, \quad DW = 0.75, \quad Mean = 110.2, \quad SEE = 13.2$$

6. Brazil (1968–85)

$$O = -77.6 + 0.604\,A + 706573.9\,RP$$
$$\quad\;\; (1.2)\;\;(4.38) \qquad\qquad (3.89)$$

$$R^2 = 0.81, \quad DW = 1.12, \quad Mean = 254, \quad SEE = 35.4$$

7. Côte d'Ivoire (1965–90)

$$O = -97.6 + 0.628\,A$$
$$\quad\;\; (2.9)(14.5)$$

$$R^2 = 0.90, \quad DW = 1.19, \quad Mean = 346.7, \quad SEE = 67.5$$

8. Rest of the world (1965–90)

$$O = 46.3 + 0.274\,A$$
$$\quad\; (1.2)\;\;(7.08)$$

$$R^2 = 0.68, \quad DW = 1.70, \quad Mean = 329, \quad SEE = 23.3$$

Key

O = output in '000 metric tonnes;
A = acreage harvested in '000 ha.;
RP = producer price in local currency deflated by local consumer price index.
$TIME$ = time trend.

A.1.2(b)   Area equations

1. Ghana (1973–90)

$$LA = 2.549 + 0.148\,LRP(-7) + 0.504\,LA(-1)$$
$$\quad\;\; (2.38)\;\;\;\; (2.58) \qquad\qquad (2.83)$$

$$R^2 = 0.72, \quad DW = 1.93, \quad Mean = 7.04, \quad SEE = 0.08$$

2. Côte d'Ivoire (1970–90)

$$LA = -2.793 + 0.404\,LRP(-4) + 0.411\,LA(-1) + 0.519\,LA(-2)$$
$$\quad\;\; (-3.75)\;\;\; (4.21) \qquad\qquad (2.25) \qquad\qquad (2.92)$$

$$R^2 = 0.99, \quad DW = 2.51, \quad Mean = 6.60, \quad SEE = 0.05$$

3. Cameroon (1975–90)

$$LA = 1.974 + 0.118\,LRP(-7) + 0.515\,LA(-1)$$
$$\quad\;\; (2.84)\;\;\;\; (1.94) \qquad\qquad (4.59)$$

$R^2 = 0.73$, $DW = 2.14$, $Mean = 6.05$, $SEE = 0.03$

4. Indonesia (1976–90)
$$LA = -7.318 + 0.872 \, LRP(-9) + 0.769 \, LA(-1)$$
$$(-3.43) \quad (3.68) \qquad\qquad (8.41)$$

$R^2 = 0.91$, $DW = 2.55$, $Mean = 3.32$, $SEE = 0.23$

5. Malaysia (1970–90)
$$LA = -2.625 + 0.920 \, LRP(-3) + 0.850 \, LA(-1)$$
$$(-2.31) \quad (2.81) \qquad\qquad (15.83)$$

$R^2 = 0.95$, $DW = 2.56$, $Mean = 4.09$, $SEE = 0.26$

6. Brazil (1975–90)
$$A = 76.67 + 483465.9 \, RP(-7) + 0.830 \, A(-1)$$
$$(1.33) \qquad (2.02) \qquad\quad (7.08)$$

$R^2 = 0.91$, $DW = 2.21$, $Mean = 556.5$, $SEE = 34.01$

Key
LA = Area harvested (1,000 *ha.*).
LRP = producer price in local currency deflated by local consumer price index.

With Brazil the only exception, all the variables are in logarithmic values.

A.1.3 *Price Equations and Closing Identities*

A.1.3(a) World price to producer price links
1. Ghana (1966–90)
$$PP = 0.397 + 0.999 \, ER + 0.798 \, WP$$
$$(0.29) \quad (18.1) \qquad (4.2)$$

$R^2 = 0.951$, $DW = 1.28$, $SEE = 0.56$, $Mean = 8.08$

2. Nigeria (1967–90)
$$PP = -0.215 + 0.514 \, ER + 0.318 \, WP + 0.712 \, PP(-1)$$
$$(0.5) \quad (5.7) \qquad (3.6) \qquad (10.7)$$

$R^2 = 0.987$, $SEE = 0.18$, $Mean = 7.02$

3. Indonesia (1968–90)

$$PP = 0.584 + 0.525\ ER + 0.405\ WP + 0.472\ PP(-1)$$

$$\quad\ (0.81)\quad (2.9)\qquad\ (3.2)\qquad\quad (3.8)$$

$$R^2 = 0.944,\quad SEE = 0.24,\quad Mean = 13.22$$

4. Malaysia (1967–90)

$$PP = 3.909 + 1.007\ ER + 0.334\ WP + 0.057\ TIME$$

$$\quad\ (3.6)\quad (2.0)\qquad\ (3.5)\qquad\ (11.5)$$

$$R^2 = 0.929,\quad DW = 1.36,\quad SEE = 0.14,\quad Mean = 8.00$$

5. Brazil (1976–89)

$$PP = -0.384 + 0.657\ ER + 0.662\ WP + 0.331\ PP(-1)$$

$$\quad\ (0.2)\quad (6.3)\qquad\ (2.1)\qquad\ (2.6)$$

$$R^2 = 0.997,\quad SEE = 0.25,\quad Mean = 0.31$$

6. Côte d'Ivoire (1966–90)

$$PP = -0.570 + 1.229\ ER + 0.786\ WP$$

$$\quad\ (0.3)\quad (3.5)\qquad\ (6.9)$$

$$R^2 = 0.752,\quad DW = 1.08,\quad SEE = 0.36,\quad Mean = 12.15$$

7. Cameroon (1966–89)

$$PP = -3.583 + 1.884\ ER + 0.683\ WP$$

$$\quad\ (1.6)\quad (4.9)\qquad\ (5.4)$$

$$R^2 = 0.741,\quad DW = 0.68,\quad SEE = 0.39,\quad Mean = 12.07$$

Key
PP = log of producer price in local currency.
ER = log of units of local currency per \$US.
WP = log of world cocoa price = Ghana spot price in London in \$US.
$TIME$ = time trend.

A.1.3(b) World price and closing identities

1. *World cocoa price equation (1964–90)*

$$LP = 1.005 + 0.307\ LCP - 0.915\ LWSTGR + 0.571\ LP(-1)$$

$$\quad\ (2.29)\qquad (3.17)\qquad (5.43)\qquad\qquad (5.70)$$

$$R^2 = 0.92,\quad DW = 1.37,\quad SEE = 0.21,\quad Mean = 7.32$$

Key
LP   = log of world cocoa price in \$US.
LCP   = log of world consumer price index.
LWSTGR = log of ratio of end of period total stocks to world
              grindings of cocoa.

2. *World grindings equation (1975–90)*
    $WGR = 109.2 + 0.982\ WCONS$

    $\qquad\quad (2.8)(41.8)$

    $R^2 = 0.99,\quad DW = 1.57,\quad SEE = 23.3,\quad Mean = 1695$

    WGR = world grindings
    $WCONS$ = world consumption

3. *World supply / demand balance identity*
    $0.99\ WS = WGR + TST - TST(-1)$

    where:

    WS = world gross crop

    TST = total world stocks at end of period

4. *Stocks identity*
    $TST = FST + BST$

    FST = free stocks at end of period

    BST = buffer stocks at end of period

5. *Consumption identity*
    $WCONS = USCONS + UKCONS + WGCONS + FRCONS$
    $\qquad\qquad\quad + JACONS + SPCONS + BECONS + SWCONS$
    $\qquad\qquad\quad + CACONS + ROWCONS$
    $\qquad\qquad\quad + SOCCONS$

    Consumption of cocoa in:
    $USCONS$ = USA
    $UKCONS$ = UK
    $WGCONS$ = West Germany
    $FRCONS$ = France
    $JACONS$ = Japan

$SPCONS = Spain$

$BECONS = Belgium$

$SWCONS = Switzerland$

$CACONS = Canada$

$SOCCONS = $ socialist countries (as of 1990)

$ROWCONS = $ Rest of the world

6. *Supply identity*

WS = Output of: Ghana, Nigeria, Indonesia, Malaysia, Cameroon, Brazil, Côte d'Ivoire, and Rest of the World

Mean = mean of consumption per capita.

A.2 The Coffee Model

A.2.1 The Demand for Coffee

1. USA (1979–90)
$$DPC = 59.047 + 2.126\ YPC(-1) - 2.652\ RCP - 1.012\ TIME$$
$$\quad\ (3.11)\quad (1.28)\qquad\qquad (1.39)\qquad\quad (1.65)$$

   $R^2 = 0.30,\quad DW = 1.64,\quad Mean = 76.95,\quad SEE = 1.99$

2. West Germany (1978–90)
$$DPC = -100.632 + 8.602\ YPC - 100.055\ RCP(-3)$$
$$\qquad\quad (1.30)\quad (4.10)\qquad\quad (1.01)$$

   $R^2 = 0.75,\quad DW = 2.25,\quad Mean = 133.69,\quad SEE = 13.62$

3. Italy (1975–90)
$$DPC = 43.045 + 2.615\ YPC - 0.061\ RCP$$
$$\qquad\ (3.57)\quad (3.81)\qquad\ (2.43)$$

   $R^2 = 0.80,\quad DW = 1.76,\quad Mean = 69.66,\quad SEE = 3.43$

4. UK (1975–90)
$$DPC = 36.720 + 2.095\ YPC - 90.323\ RCP$$
$$\qquad\ (3.72)\quad (1.47)\qquad\ (2.69)$$

   $R^2 = 0.43,\quad DW = 1.70,\quad Mean = 39.08,\quad SEE = 3.43$

5. France (1976–90)
$$DPC = -41.104 + 1.90\ YPC(-1) - 13.093\ D(RCP)$$
$$\qquad\quad (0.81)\quad (2.66)\qquad\qquad (2.18)$$
$$\qquad\qquad\quad -2.602\ TIME$$
$$\qquad\qquad\quad\ (2.57)$$

   $R^2 = 0.63,\quad DW = 1.96,\quad Mean = 94.79,\quad SEE = 3.08$

6. Spain (1977–90)
$$DPC = -20.859 + 0.108\ YPC - 0.743\ RCP$$
$$\qquad\quad (1.14)\quad (5.06)\qquad\ (2.04)$$

   $R^2 = 0.81,\quad DW = 2.81,\quad Mean = 52.47,\quad SEE = 4.94$

7. Netherlands (1975–90)

$$DPC = 87.823 + 3.714\ YPC - 242.895\ RCP$$
$$\quad (1.21)\quad (1.58)\qquad\qquad (3.18)$$

$$R^2 = 0.58,\quad DW = 1.63,\quad Mean = 151.32,\quad SEE = 13.04$$

8. Japan (1975–90)

$$DPC = -2.927 + 0.018\ YCP - 0.276\ RCP$$
$$\quad (0.35)\quad 9.43)\qquad\quad (2.13)$$

$$R^2 = 0.93,\quad DW = 2.00,\quad Mean = 32.83,\quad SEE = 2.45$$

9. Brazil (1973–90)

$$DPC = 64.387 + 614.830\ YCP - 898.759\ RCP - 0.929\ TIME$$
$$\quad (11.67)\qquad (1.31)\qquad\qquad (2.12)\qquad\qquad (5.49)$$

$$R^2 = 0.72,\quad DW = 1.58,\quad Mean = 60.12,\quad SEE = 3.52$$

Key

DPC = consumption of cocoa ('000 tonnes) per capita (million).

YPC = real GNP per capita in 1985 prices.

RCP = real cocoa price (Ghana spot price in London times exchange rate divided by consumer price index).

RSP = real sugar price (raw sugar price in London times exchange rate divided by consumer price index).

$TIME$ = time trend.

$Mean$ = mean of consumption per capita.

A.2.2   The Production of Coffee

A.2.2(a)   Output equations

1. Brazil (1974–90)

$$Q = -19499.9 + 16.899\ A + 920733.12\ RP(-1) - 875.20\ TIME$$
$$\qquad\quad (1.95)\ (3.47)\qquad (2.76)\qquad\qquad (1.85)$$

$$R^2 = 0.74,\quad DW = 2.37,\quad Mean = 23300.82,\quad SEE = 2950.41$$

2. Colombia (1967–90)

$$Q = -12387.46 + 25.280\ A$$
$$\qquad (3.80)\quad (7.08)$$

$$R^2 = 0.69,\quad DW = 1.49,\quad Mean = 10571.33,\quad SEE = 1372.89$$

3. Indonesia (1967–90)
$$Q = 129.66 + 9.942\,A$$
$$(0.644)(23.71)$$

$R^2 = 0.96,\quad DW = 1.30,\quad Mean = 4634.17,\quad SEE = 327.74$

4. Mexico (1967–90)
$$Q = -1146.69 + 13.62\,A$$
$$(0.984)\ (4.530)$$

$R^2 = 0.48,\quad DW = 1.15,\quad Mean = 4098.33,\quad SEE = 618.74$

5. Côte d'Ivoire (1973–90)
$$Q = -4090.55 + 3.515\,A + 1246.52\,RP$$
$$(1.49)\ (2.05)\qquad (3.19)$$

$R^2 = 0.42,\quad DW = 2.25,\quad Mean = 4215.61,\quad SEE = 818.31$

6. India (1967–90)
$$Q = -583.88 + 14.307\,A$$
$$(1.01)\ \ (4.50)$$

$R^2 = 0.48,\quad DW = 3.37,\quad Mean = 1958.62,\quad SEE = 561.84$

7. Guatemala (1967–90)
$$Q = 382.24 + 9.551\,A$$
$$(1.19)\ (6.79)$$

$R^2 = 0.68,\quad DW = 0.94,\quad Mean = 2526.79,\quad SEE = 258.21$

8. Uganda (1967–90)
$$Q = -464.05 + 12.214\,A - 69.384\,TIME$$
$$(0.58)\ \ (4.56)\qquad (4.16)$$

$R^2 = 0.54,\quad DW = 2.58,\quad Mean = 2771.29,\quad SEE = 465.66$

Key

Q = output in '000 bags.

A = acreage harvested in '000 ha.;

RP = real producer price of coffee (producer price in local currency deflated by local consumer price index).

$TIME$ = time trend.

$Mean$ = mean of output.

A.2.2(b)   Area equations
1. Brazil (1978–90)

$$A = 1830.18 + 45450.97\ RP(-5) + 83.416\ TIME$$
$$\quad\ (15.48)\qquad (2.36)\qquad\qquad (12.65)$$

$$R^2 = 0.94,\quad DW = 1.11,\quad Mean = 2956.46,\quad SEE = 88.95$$

2. Colombia (1976–90)

$$A = 878.27 + 0.146\ RP(-3) + 4.381\ TIME$$
$$\quad\ (33.0)\quad (1.93)\qquad\qquad (3.51)$$

$$R^2 = 0.53,\quad DW = 2.09,\quad Mean = 960.8, SEE = 20.24$$

3. Indonesia (1982–90)

$$A = 231.29 + 3.017\ RP(-9) + 26.741\ TIME$$
$$\quad\ (5.96)\ (2.33)\qquad\qquad (10.39)$$

$$R^2 = 0.95,\quad DW = 2.11,\quad Mean = 623.22,\quad SEE = 19.93$$

4. Mexico (1983–90)

$$A = 368.14 + 0.234\ RP(-10)$$
$$\quad\ (10.03)\ (1.77)$$

$$R^2 = 0.34,\quad DW = 1.11,\quad Mean = 429.25,\quad SEE = 35.73$$

5. India (1979–90)

$$A = 152.92 + 0.952\ RP(-6) + 3.967\ TIME$$
$$\quad\ (49.0)\quad (5.11)\qquad\qquad (23.29)$$

$$R^2 = 0.98,\quad DW = 2.03,\quad Mean = 209.74,\quad SEE = 2.029$$

6. Guatemala (1978–90)

$$A = 226.05 + 15.029\ RP(-5) + 0.985\ TIME$$
$$\quad\ (23.34)\ (2.89)\qquad\qquad (2.67)$$

$$R^2 = 0.51,\quad DW = 1.23,\quad Mean = 256.69,\quad SEE = 4.26$$

Key
A = acreage harvested in '000 ha.;
RP = real producer price of coffee (producer price in local currency deflated by local consumer price index).
$TIME$ = time trend.
Mean = mean of area harvested.

A.2.3 Price Equations and Closing Identities

A.2.3(a) World price to retail price links

1. West Germany (1975–90)

$$LRP = 0.884 + 0.218\,LER + 0.383\,LWPR + 0.007\,TIME$$
$$\quad\;(2.99)\quad(2.24)\qquad\;\;(6.63)\qquad\qquad(1.86)$$

$$R^2 = 0.82, \quad DW = 1.70, \quad Mean = 2.96, \quad SEE = 0.06$$

2. France (1976–90)

$$LRP = -0.157 + 0.532\,LER + 0.347\,LWPR + 0.310\,LRP(-1)$$
$$\qquad\;\;(0.23)\quad(4.20)\qquad\;\;(3.34)\qquad\qquad(3.39)$$

$$R^2 = 0.82, \quad Mean = 3.57, \quad SEE = 0.10$$

3. The Netherlands (1975–90)

$$LRP = -1.306 + 0.166\,LER + 0.748\,LWPR + 0.028\,TIME$$
$$\qquad\;\;(4.03)\quad(1.58)\qquad(11.67)\qquad\qquad(6.83)$$

$$R^2 = 0.93, \quad DW = 1.79, \quad Mean = 2.67, \quad SEE = 0.07$$

4. Spain (1977–90)

$$LRP = 0.506 + 0.326\,LER + 0.857\,LWPR + 0.072\,TIME$$
$$\quad\;(0.46)\quad(1.98)\qquad\;\;(3.88)\qquad\qquad(3.87)$$

$$R^2 = 0.84, \quad DW = 2.10, \quad Mean = 6.68, \quad SEE = 0.13$$

5. Japan (1975–90)

$$LRP = 4.074 + 0.244\,LER + 0.494\,LWPR + 0.035\,TIME$$
$$\quad\;(5.15)\quad(1.91)\qquad\;\;(7.83)\qquad\qquad(4.66)$$

$$R^2 = 0.86, \quad DW = 1.98, \quad Mean = 8.03, \quad SEE = 0.07$$

6. USA (1975–90)

$$LRP = 2.039 + 0.643\,LWPR + 0.054\,TIME$$
$$\quad\;(3.88)\quad(6.18)\qquad\;\;(7.46)$$

$$R^2 = 0.84, \quad DW = 0.97, \quad Mean = 5.51, \quad SEE = 0.11$$

7. UK (1976–90)

$$LRP = 0.405 + 0.470\,LER + 0.339\,LWPR(-1) + 0.058\,TIME$$
$$\quad\;(0.64)\quad(2.01)\qquad\;\;(2.71)\qquad\qquad\;\;(6.79)$$

$$R^2 = 0.87, \quad DW = 2.42, \quad Mean = 2.26, \quad SEE = 0.13$$

8. Italy (1976–90)

$$LRP = 5.989 + 0.190\ LER + 0.291\ LWPR(-1) + 0.060\ TIME$$
$$\qquad\quad (4.96)\quad (1.21)\qquad\quad (2.47)\qquad\qquad\quad (5.97)$$

$$R^2 = 0.89,\quad DW = 2.27,\quad Mean = 9.23,\quad SEE = 012$$

Key

LRP = log of nominal retail price in local currency.
LER = log of units of local currency per \$US.
$LWPR$ = log of world coffee price (composite indicator price, ICO).
$TIME$ = time trend.

A.2.3(b)   World price to producer price links

1. Brazil (1973–90)

$$LPP = -6.506 + 0.942\ LER + 0.834\ LWPR$$
$$\qquad\quad (4.51)\quad (45.81)\qquad (2.83)$$

$$R^2 = 0.99,\quad DW = 2.16,\quad Mean = 4.09,\quad SEE = 0.43$$

2. Colombia (1973–90)

$$LPP = 1.537 + 1.123\ LER + 0.624\ LWPR$$
$$\qquad\quad (3.83)\quad (38.98)\qquad (7.99)$$

$$R^2 = 0.99,\quad DW = 1.42,\quad Mean = 9.44,\quad SEE = 0.12$$

3. Indonesia (1973–90)

$$LPP = -3.975 + 0.930\ LER + 0.937\ LWPR$$
$$\qquad\quad (3.65)\quad (8.70)\qquad (5.48)$$

$$R^2 = 0.88,\quad DW = 1.61,\quad Mean = 6.73,\quad SEE = 0.25$$

4. Mexico (1973–90)

$$LPP = 2.246 + 0.813\ LER + 0.456\ LWPR + 0.078\ TIME$$
$$\qquad\quad (2.75)\quad (8.99)\qquad (2.94)\qquad\quad (2.26)$$

$$R^2 = 0.99,\quad DW = 1.50,\quad Mean = 8.81,\quad SEE = 0.20$$

5. India (1974–90)

$$LPP = 0.698 + 0.911\ LER + 0.518\ LWPR + 0.216\ LPP(-1)$$
$$\qquad\quad (1.06)\quad (4.99)\qquad (5.00)\qquad\quad (1.82)$$

$$R^2 = 0.89,\quad Mean = 6.77,\quad SEE = 0.12$$

6. Guatemala (1973–90)

$$LPP = 1.597 + 0.706\,LER + 0.533\,LWPR + 0.032\,TIME$$
$$(2.41)\quad(4.55)\qquad(3.67)\qquad\quad(2.09)$$

$$R^2 = 0.91,\quad DW = 1.36,\quad Mean = 4.63,\quad SEE = 0.18$$

7. Côte d'Ivoire (1973–90)

$$LPP = -2.484 + 1.071\,LER + 0.414\,LWPR$$
$$(1.28)\quad(3.32)\qquad(1.91)$$

$$R^2 = 0.53,\quad DW = 0.75,\quad Mean = 5.53,\quad SEE = 0.32$$

Key
LPP = log of nominal producer price in local currency.
LER = log of units of local currency per \$US.
$LWPR$= log of world cocoa price (composite indicator price, ICO).
$TIME$ = time trend.

A.2.3(c)   World price and closing identities
1. *World coffee price equation (1968–90)*

$$LP = 1.468 - 0.789\,LPSTRT + 0.591\,LP(-1)$$
$$(3.19)\quad(2.7)\qquad\qquad(4.78)$$

$$R^2 = 0.84,\quad Mean = 4.55,\quad SEE = 0.218$$

where:
LP = log of world coffee price
$LSTRT$ = log of ratio of producer stocks to world coffee production

2. *Link equation (1968–90)*

$$LCST = 10.518 - 0.129\,LP(-1)$$
$$(75.12)\quad(4.19)$$

$$R^2 = 0.45,\quad DW = 1.38,\quad Mean = 9.93,\quad SEE = 0.081$$

where:
$LCST$ = log of consumer stocks.
LP = log of world coffee price.

3. *Identities*
    - *Consumption identities*

    $$WCONS = USCONS + WGCONS + ITCONS$$
    $$+ UKCONS + FRCONS + SPCONS$$
    $$+ NECONS + JACONS + BRCONS$$
    $$+ RWCONS$$
    $$MC = USCONS + WGCONS + ITCONS$$
    $$+ UKCONS + FRCONS + SPCONS$$
    $$+ NECONS + JACONS + RWMC$$
    $$PC = BRCONS + RWPC$$
    $$RWCONS = RWMC + RWPC$$

    - *Supply identity*

    $$WP = BRPROD + COLPROD + INDOPROD$$
    $$+ MEXPROD + IVPROD + INDIPROD$$
    $$+ GUAPROD + UGAPROD + RWWP$$

    - *Stock identities*

    $$DPST = WP - PC - NMC - E$$
    $$R + DCST = X - MC$$
    $$DPST = PST_t - PST_{t-1}$$
    $$DCST = CST_t - CST_{t-1}$$
    $$DCST = CST_t - CST_{t-1}$$
    $$PSTRT = PST/WP$$
    $$X = E + N$$
    $$NMCRT = NMC/PC + MC$$

Model variables

WP	= world coffee production
WCONS	= world coffee consumption
A	= acreage
PC	= consumption by producers
MC	= importing member consumption
RWCONS	= rest of world consumption
RWPC	= rest of world PC
RWMC	= rest of world MC

RWWP	= rest of world production
PST	= producer stocks
CST	= consumer stocks
P	= world coffee price
PP	= producer price
RPP	= real producer price
RP	= retail price
RRP	= real retail price
NMC	= exports to non-members from member countries
E	= exports to member countries from member countries
N	= exports to member countries from non-members
R	= re-exports by importing members to all destinations
X	= imports of member countries from all sources
USCONS	= USA consumption of coffee
WGCONS	= West Germany consumption
ITCONS	= Italy consumption
UKCONS	= UK consumption
FRCONS	= France consumption
SPCONS	= Spain consumption
NECONS	= Netherlands consumption
JACONS	= Japan consumption
BRCONS	= Brazil consumption
BRPROD	= Brazil production
COLPROD	= Colombia production
INDOPROD	= Indonesia production
MEXPROD	= Mexico production
IVPROD	= Ivory Coast production
INDIPROD	= India production
GUAPROD	= Guatemala production
UGAPROD	= Uganda production

A.3 The Tea Model

A.3.1 The Demand For Tea

1. India (1966–77 and 1979–90)
$$CPC = 82.259 + 133.83\ YPC - 309.28\ D(RRTP)$$
$$\quad(1.87)\qquad(9.53)\qquad\quad(2.00)$$

$$R^2 = 0.81,\quad DW = 1.49,\quad Mean = 493.60,\quad SEE = 35.54$$

2. USA (1963–91)
$$LCPC = 4.955 - 0.466\ LRRTP$$
$$\quad(13.50)\quad(2.39)$$

$$R^2 = 0.18,\quad DW = 2.06,\quad Mean = 5.834,\quad SEE = 0.08$$

3. UK (1974–91)
$$LCPC = 8.388 - 0.170\ LRRTP - 0.015\ TIME$$
$$\quad(131.21)\quad(3.55)\qquad\quad(9.00)$$

$$R^2 = 0.90,\quad DW = 2.57,\quad Mean = 8.02,\quad SEE = 0.033$$

4. China (1974–89)
$$LCPC = 5.907 + 0.697\ LYPC$$
$$\quad(88.06)\quad(7.83)$$

$$R^2 = 0.81,\quad DW = 0.81,\quad Mean = 5.43,\quad SEE = 0.11$$

5. Iran (1964–90)
$$LCPC = 5.873 + 0.242\ LYPC - 0.233\ LRTP$$
$$\quad(7.04)\quad(1.67)\qquad\quad(4.97)$$

$$R^2 = 0.52,\quad DW = 1.24,\quad Mean = 7.00,\quad SEE = 0.19$$

6. Pakistan (1972–91)
$$LCPC = 5.515 + 0.799\ LYPC$$
$$\quad(29.83)\quad(6.44)$$

$$R^2 = 0.70,\quad DW = 1.76,\quad Mean = 6.697,\quad SEE = 0.09$$

7. Japan (1963–91)

$$LCPC = 2.605 + 0.639 \, LYPC - 0.091 \, LRTP - 0.029 \, TIME$$
$$ (3.99) \quad (7.25) \qquad\quad (2.63) \qquad\qquad (7.61)$$

$$R^2 = 0.80, \quad DW = 2.14, \quad Mean = 6.86, \quad SEE = 0.04$$

8. Turkey (1963–90)

$$LCPC = -10.964 + 2.929 \, LYPC$$
$$ (6.96) \quad (11.4)$$

$$R^2 = 0.83, \quad DW = 1.47, \quad Mean = 7.01, \quad SEE = 0.31$$

9. Indonesia (1967–91)

$$LCPC = 0.303 + 1.118 \, LYPC - 0.663 \, LRTP$$
$$ (0.15) \quad (5.07) \qquad\quad (2.11)$$

$$R^2 = 0.66, \quad DW = 0.97, \quad Mean = 5.03, \quad SEE = 0.33$$

10. Kenya (1967–89)

$$LCPC = -26.31 + 3.747 \, LYPC - 0.88 \, LRTP(-2)$$
$$ (2.55) \quad (3.01) \qquad\quad (1.66)$$

$$R^2 = 0.52, \quad DW = 1.61, \quad Mean = 6.27, \quad SEE = 0.52$$

11. Egypt (1974–91)

$$LCPC = -1.438 + 1.236 \, LYPC - 0.159 \, LRTP$$
$$ (0.86) \quad (5.06) \qquad\quad (1.99)$$

$$R^2 = 0.64, \quad DW = 2.07, \quad Mean = 7.15, \quad SEE = 0.15$$

12. Rest of the world (1972–89)

$$LRWM = 10.410 + 0.527 \, LWGDPI$$
$$ (28.75) \quad (6.52)$$

$$R^2 = 0.73, \quad DW = 1.59, \quad Mean = 12.76, \quad SEE = 0.05$$

Key

LCPC	= log of tea consumption (metric tonnes) per capita (million).
LYPC	= log of real GNP per capita in 1985 prices.
LRRTP	= log of real retail price of tea (retail price in national currency divided by consumer price index).

LRTP = log of real tea price (world price times exchange rate
         divided by consumer price index).
TIME = time trend.
Mean = mean of consumption per capita.

A.3.2   The Production of Tea: Yield Equations

1. India (1978–91)
$$Y = 2903.42 - 4.70\,A + 946.26\,RPP(-1) + 39.57\,TIME$$
$$\quad\;\;(4.37)\;(2.58)\qquad(3.41)\qquad\qquad(6.09)$$

   $R^2 = 0.91,\quad DW = 1.80\quad Mean = 1573.66,\quad SEE = 39.35$

2. China (1971–91)
$$Y = 669.88 - 0.567\,A + 2000.2\,RPP(-4) + 18.21\,TIME$$
$$\quad\;\;(10.53)\;(7.80)\qquad(2.34)\qquad\qquad(7.15)$$

   $R^2 = 0.84,\quad DW = 1.41,\quad Mean = 356.33,\quad SEE = 42.48$

3. Kenya (1963–91)
$$Y = 807.64 - 34.11\,A + 1019.87\,RPP(-1) + 149.29\,TIME$$
$$\quad\;\;(4.80)\;(7.12)\qquad(3.44)\qquad\qquad(9.57)$$

   $R^2 = 0.91,\quad DW = 2.52,\quad Mean = 1442.06,\quad SEE = 118.91$

4. Turkey (1964–91)
$$Y = 749.76 - 27.21\,A + 39.23\,RPP(-2) + 111.96\,TIME$$
$$\quad\;\;(2.97)\;(2.13)\qquad(1.67)\qquad\qquad(2.98)$$

   $R^2 = 0.56,\quad DW = 1.28,\quad Mean = 1342.2,\quad SEE = 273.2$

5. Japan (1963–91)
$$Y = 2107.24 - 8.03\,A$$
$$\quad\;\;(11.35)\;(2.46)$$

   $R^2 = 0.18,\quad DW = 0.90,\quad Mean = 1651.9,\quad SEE = 83.52$

6. Iran (1963–91)
$$Y = 15.65 + 30.71\,A$$
$$\quad\;\;(0.05)\;\;(2.93)$$

   $R^2 = 0.24,\quad DW = 1.13,\quad Mean = 920.06,\quad SEE = 277.09$

7. Indonesia (1963–91)

$$Y = -171.28 + 4.87\,A(-1) + 49.95\,TIME$$
$$(0.65)\quad(1.73)\qquad\quad(17.28)$$

$$R^2 = 0.92,\quad DW = 1.63,\quad Mean = 958.9,\quad SEE = 124.2$$

Key

Y	= yield (kg/A).
A	= real producer price (world tea price times exchange rate divided by consumer price index; for India only, the local price deflated by local consumer price index, was used).
$TIME$	= time trend.
$Mean$	= mean of yield.

A.3.3 'Rest of World' Exports

$$RWX = 100717.7 + 415.31\,RWA + 2713.97\,TIME$$
$$(1.96)\qquad(3.91)\qquad\qquad(4.78)$$

$$R^2 = 0.90,\quad DW = 1.83,\quad Mean = 355782.2,\quad SEE = 13580.2$$

Key

RWX	= rest of world exports in metric tonnes.
RWA	= rest of world area harvested in '000 ha.
$TIME$	= time trend.
$Mean$	= mean of rest of world exports.

Definitions

RWX = World Exports —(India Exports + China Exports
+ Indonesia Exports + Iran Exports
+ Kenya Exports + Japan Exports + Turkey Exports).

RWA = World Area Harvested —(India Area + China Area
+ Indonesia Area + Iran Area + Kenya Area
+ Japan Area + Turkey Area).

A.3.4 World Price, UK stocks, and Closing Identities

A.3.4(a) World price to retail price links

1. India (1965–91)

$$LRP = 1.106 + 0.530\ LER + 0.239\ LWPR + 0.051\ TIME$$
$$\quad\quad (3.93)\quad (3.36)\quad\quad\quad (2.54)\quad\quad\quad\quad (6.12)$$

$$R^2 = 0.98, \quad DW = 1.66, \quad Mean = 3.083, \quad SEE = 0.095$$

2. UK (1975–91)

$$LRP = 2.357 + 0.17\ LER + 0.352\ LWPR + 0.035\ TIME$$
$$\quad\quad (2.79)\quad (0.57)\quad\quad (1.71)\quad\quad\quad\quad (1.72)$$
$$\quad + 0.523\ LRP(-1)$$
$$\quad\quad (2.89)$$

$$R^2 = 0.93, \quad Mean = 5.818, \quad SEE = 0.152$$

3. USA (1963–91)

$$LRP = 0.447 + 0.135\ LWPR + 0.014\ TIME + 0.682\ LRP(-1)$$
$$\quad\quad (4.71)\quad (4.38)\quad\quad\quad (4.04)\quad\quad\quad (9.70)$$

$$R^2 = 0.99, \quad Mean = 2.183, \quad SEE = 0.034$$

Key
LRP   = log of nominal retail price in local currency.
LER   = log of units of local currency per \$US.
LWPR   = log of world tea price.
TIME   = time trend.

A.3.4(b) World price to producer price links

1. India (1977–91)

$$PP = -16.057 + 1.684\ ER + 6.47\ WPR + 1.185\ TIME$$
$$\quad\quad (3.03)\quad (3.74)\quad\quad (3.43)\quad\quad (2.73)$$

$$R^2 = 0.95, \quad DW = 2.42, \quad Mean = 26.58, \quad SEE = 2.89$$

Key
PP   = nominal producer price in local currency.
ER   = units of local currency per \$US.
WPR   = world tea price.
TIME   = time trend.

A.3.4(c)   UK tea stocks (1970–90)

$$WPR = 1.362 - 3.651\ UKSTRT + 0.417\ WPR(-1)$$

$$(4.43)\quad (2.35)\qquad\qquad (4.12)$$

$$+1.127\ D77 + 1.434\ D84$$

$$(4.64)\qquad\quad (5.79)$$

$$R^2 = 0.87,\quad Mean = 1.869,\quad SEE = 0.235$$

Key

WPR	= world tea price (\$US per kg).
UKSTRT	= total UK stocks to world exports ratio.
D77	= dummy variable for 1977.
D84	= dummy variable for 1984
Mean	= mean of world tea price.

Identities

$$JAM = JAC - JAP + JAX$$

$$IRANM = IRANC - IRANP + IRANX$$

$$WM = UKM + PAKM + USM + EGM + IRANM$$
$$+ USSRM + JAM + RWM$$

$$WM = WX - E$$

$$WX = INDIX + CHX + INDOX + IRANX + KEX$$
$$+ JAX + TUX + RWX$$

$$INDIX = INDIP - INDIC$$

$$CHX = CHP - CHC$$

$$INDOX = INDOP - INDOC$$

$$KEX = KEP - KEC$$

$$TUX = TUP - TUC$$

$$UKST = UKM - UKC + UKST(-1)$$

Prefix definitions

JA = Japan, $IRAN$ = Iran, UK = UK, PAK = Pakistan,

US = USA, EG = Egypt, $USSR$ = USSR,

RW = Rest of the world, W = World, $INDI$ = India,

CH = China, $INDO$ = Indonesia, KE = Kenya, TU = Turkey

Suffix definitions
M = Imports, X = Exports, P = Production,
C = Apparent consumption, ST = Stock levels,
E = Balancing error.

Exogenous Vriables
JAX, IRANX, E, USSRM, RWM

B. Simulation results

B.1 Simulation results for cocoa, 1985–1990[a]

	1985	1986	1987	1988	1989	1990
Production ('000 tonnes)						
Base case	1,872	1,957	2,040	2,266	2,383	2,324
Stock reduction	1,760	1,806	1,851	1,953	2,173	2,227
Production cut-back:						
Smaller	2,198	1,647	1,950	1,954	2,209	1,904
Larger	2,048	1,724	1,919	1,923	2,169	1,883
Export tax	1,865	1,938	2,006	2,104	2,266	2,163
Consumption ('000 tonnes)						
Base case	1,727	1,709	1,809	1,853	2,041	1,951
Stock reduction	1,717	1,658	1,720	1,740	1,932	1,855
Poduction cut-back						
Smaller	1,745	1,764	1,826	1,830	1,986	1,878
Larger	1,739	1,740	1,799	1,802	1,957	1,851
Export tax	1,727	1,706	1,803	1,842	2,027	1,932
Stocks ('000 tonnes)						
Base case	493	643	777	993	1,238	1,513
Stock reduction	393	443	447	593	738	913
Production cut-back						
Smaller	800	589	617	644	772	702
Larger	657	535	559	585	701	637
Export tax						
Price ($ per tonne)						
Base case	3,397	3,033	2,581	1,996	1,606	1,205
Stock reduction	4,157	4,664	4,936	4,388	3,855	3,018
Production cut-back						
Smaller	2,202	2,638	2,971	3,175	3,150	3,457
Larger	2,628	3,148	3,545	3,790	3,759	4,126
Export tax	3,433	3,146	2,791	2,290	2,032	1,727
Export revenue ($ bn.)						
Base case	5.16	4.81	4.32	3.56	3.23	2.32
Stock reduction	5.85	6.69	7.31	6.89	6.90	5.21
Production cut-back						
Smaller	4.07	3.37	6.69	4.90	5.75	5.20
Larger	4.46	4.22	5.50	5.84	6.72	6.12
Export tax	5.20	4.93	4.57	3.94	3.83	3.05

[a] See Table 5.2 for assumptions made for changes in stocks, production, and export tax.

B.2   *Simulation results for coffee, 1983–1990[a]*

	1983	1984	1985	1986	1987	1988	1989	1990
Production (million bags)								
Base case	85.7	88.4	83.0	95.3	98.5	92.7	93.3	95.3
Production cut:								
Smaller	82.8	85.3	80.2	92.0	95.1	89.6	90.2	92.0
Larger	80.0	82.3	77.3	88.7	91.7	86.6	87.1	88.8
Export quota cut-back								
Smaller	85.7	88.4	83.0	95.3	98.5	92.7	93.3	95.3
Larger	85.7	88.4	83.0	95.3	98.5	92.7	93.3	95.3
Consumption (million bags)								
Base case	72.6	77.2	75.5	76.8	77.8	80.1	81.5	81.1
Production cut:								
Smaller	75.6	77.0	75.0	76.0	76.8	78.9	79.9	79.2
Larger	75.5	76.7	74.3	74.7	75.4	77.1	77.4	76.1
Export quota cut-back								
Smaller	75.4	77.0	75.4	76.4	76.7	78.4	79.8	79.0
Larger	75.0	76.6	74.9	75.8	76.1	77.8	79.1	78.4
Stocks (million bags)								
Base case	69.1	67.8	63.5	65.8	79.4	77.9	73.0	72.7
Production cut:								
Smaller	66.2	62.1	55.6	55.3	66.5	63.2	56.7	55.0
Larger	63.4	56.6	47.8	45.5	54.7	50.1	43.0	41.3
Export quota cut-back:								
Smaller	69.3	68.2	64.1	66.7	81.5	81.7	78.5	80.3
Larger	69.7	69.0	65.3	68.5	83.8	84.7	82.1	84.5
Export quantity (million bags)								
Base case	61.7	58.2	59.1	63.0	53.4	60.6	67.6	64.7
Production cut:								
Smaller	61.6	58.0	58.5	62.0	52.2	59.3	65.8	62.6
Larger	61.6	57.7	57.6	60.4	50.5	57.4	63.1	59.2
Export quota cut-back:								
Smaller	61.4	57.8	59.1	62.7	52.0	58.3	65.4	62.7
Larger	61.0	57.0	58.7	62.1	51.4	57.7	64.8	62.0
Price (US cents per lb)								
Base case	116	117	120	131	115	104	106	109
Production cut:								
Smaller	119	127	144	172	157	151	169	189
Larger	121	140	178	240	229	238	297	358
Export quota cut-back:								
Smaller	130	125	125	150	169	181	179	197
Larger	150	144	144	173	195	208	201	227

	1983	1984	1985	1986	1987	1988	1989	1990
Export revenue ($ bn.)								
Base case	7.20	6.85	7.15	8.30	6.16	6.31	7.18	7.10
Production cut:								
Smaller	7.34	7.40	8.43	10.69	8.23	9.00	11.16	11.86
Larger	7.49	8.09	10.29	14.56	11.61	13.68	18.77	21.21
Export quota cut-back:								
Smaller	7.98	7.25	7.42	9.43	8.81	10.56	11.75	12.37
Larger	9.15	8.26	8.50	10.79	10.05	12.05	13.43	14.12

[a] See Table 5.5 for assumptions made for changes in production and exports.

B.3 Simulation results for tea, 1986–1990[a]

	1986	1987	1988	1989	1990
Export quantity (1,000 tonnes)					
Base case	999	946	1,004	996	1,013
Export quota cut-back					
Smaller	985	932	992	1,009	1,007
Larger	977	923	982	999	996
Export tax	972	923	975	959	951
Price ($ per tonne)					
Base case	2,000	1,850	2,025	2,160	2,670
Export quota cut-back					
Smaller	2,285	2,573	2,751	2,729	2,995
Larger	2,665	3,001	3,208	3,182	3,493
Export tax	2,000	1,910	2,210	2,520	3,240
Export revenue ($ m.)					
Base case	1,998	1,750	2,034	2,152	2,705
Export quota cut-back					
Smaller	2,250	2,397	2,729	2,754	3,017
Larger	2,604	2,769	3,150	3,178	3,481
Export tax	1,949	1,758	2,156	2,419	3,081

[a] See Table 5.8 for assumptions made for changes in exports and export tax.

References

Adams, F. G., and J. R. Behrman (1976), 'Econometric Modelling of the Cocoa Market' in J. Simmons (ed.), *Cocoa Production: Economic and Botanical Perspectives*, New York, Praeger Publishers.

Ady, P. (1968), 'Supply Functions in Tropical Agriculture', *Oxford Bulletin of Economics and Statistics*, University of Oxford

Akiyama, T., and R. C. Duncan (1982), 'Analysis of the World Coffee Market', World Bank Staff *Commodity Working Papers*, 7, World Bank, Washington, DC.

————(1984), 'Analysis of the World Cocoa Market', World Bank Staff *Commodity Working Papers*, 8, Washington, DC.

——and P. K. Trivedi (1987), 'A New Global Tea Model: Specification, Estimation and Simulation', World Bank Staff *Commodity Working Papers*, 17, World Bank, Washington, DC.

——and P. N. Varangis (1989), 'Impact of the International Coffee Agreement's Export Quota System on the World's Coffee Market', *World Bank Working Paper* 148, World Bank, Washington, DC.

————(1990), 'The Impact of the International Coffee Agreement on Producing Countries', *World Bank Economic Review*, vol. 2: 157–73, World Bank, Washington, DC.

Bateman, M. J. (1965), 'Aggregate and Regional Supply Functions for Ghanaian Cocoa: 1946–63', *Journal of Farm Economics*, 47.

Behrman, J. R. (1965), 'Cocoa: A Study of Demand Elasticities in the Five Leading Consuming Countries, 1950–1961', *Journal of Farm Economics*, 47.

——(1968), 'Monopolistic Cocoa Pricing', *American Journal of Agricultural Economics*, 50.

Berndt, E. R. (1991), *The Practice of Econometrics*, Addison Wesley, New York.

Borensztein, E., and C. M. Reinhart (1994), 'The Macroeconomic Determinants of Real Commodity Prices', *Staff Papers*, 41, (June), International Monetary Fund, Washington, DC.

Chung, C., and G. Ukpong (1981),'The World Tea Economy: An Econometric Model of its Structure, Performance and Prospects', in *World Bank Commodity Models*, 1, World Bank Staff *Commodity Working Paper*, 6, World Bank, Washington, DC.

Cramer, J. S. (1991) *The Logit Model*, Edward Arnold, London.

226 *References*

Esfahani, H. S. (1991), 'Exports, Imports and Economic Growth in Semi-Industrialised Countries', *Journal of Development Economics*, (Jan).

Friedheim, T. (1992), 'Price Analysis of the World Tea Market', *Diskussionsschriften*, Forschungsstelle für Internationale Agrarentwicklung E. V., Heidelberg.

Gilbert, C. L. (1987), 'International Commodity Agreements: Design and Performance', *World Development*, 15/5.

Gordon-Ashworth, F. (1984), *International Commodity Control: A Contemporary History and Appraisal*, London, Croom Helm

Government of Ceylon (1974), *Report of the Commission on the Agency Houses and Brokering Firms*, Ceylon Sessional Papers.

Grilli, E. R. and M. C. Yang (1988), 'Primary Commodity Prices, Manufactured Goods Prices, and the Terms of Trade of Developing Countries: What the Long Run Shows', *World Bank Economic Review*, 2, World Bank, Washington, DC.

Groenendaal, W. J. H., and J. W. A. Vingerhoets (1988), 'The New Cocoa Agreement Analysed', Tilburg University, Dept. of Economics, *Research Memorandum*, 339 (June).

Lord, M. J. (1991), *Imperfect Competition and International Commodity Trade*, Clarendon Press, Oxford.

Maizels, A. (1992), *Commodities in Crisis*, Clarendon Press, Oxford.

OECD (1980), *Economic Outlook*, 27, Paris.

Sarkar, G. K. (1972), *The World Tea Economy*, Oxford University Press, Delhi.

Simmons, J., and Miranowski, J. (1976), 'Economics of Cocoa Production', in J. Simmons (ed.) *Cocoa Production, Economic and Botanical Perspectives*, New York, Praeger Publishers.

Spraos (1983), *Inequalising Trade? A Study of Traditional North/South Specialisation in the Context of Terms of Trade Concepts*, Clarendon Press, Oxford, in co-operation with UNCTAD.

UNCTAD (1981), *The Processing before Export of Cocoa: Areas for International Co-Operation*, Geneva, (TD/B. C.1/PSC/18), mimeo.

—— (1982*a*), The Marketing and Processing of Tea: Areas for International Co-Operation (document TD/B/C.1/PSC/28, 7 Dec.).

—— (1982*b*), Report of the Third Preparatory Meeting on Tea, Geneva, (TD/B/IPC/TEA/14), mimeo.

—— (1982*c*), The Marketing and Processing of Tea: Areas for International Co-Operation), Geneva, (TD/B/C.1/PSC/28), mimeo.

—— (1983), The Processing, Marketing and Distribution of Coffee: Areas for International Co-Operation, Geneva (TD/B/C.1/PSC/31/Rev. 1), mimeo.

—— (1984), *The Processing and Marketing of Coffee: Areas for International Co-operation*, Oxford University Press, New York.

—— (1985), The Role of International Commodity Agreements or Arrangements in Attaining the Objectives of the Integrated Programme for Commodities, Geneva (TD/B/C.1/270), mimeo.

—— (1989, 1992, 1994), *Commodity Yearbook*, New York, United Nations

—— (1993), press release, 'UN Conference adopts new International Cocoa Agreement'.

UNCTAD/ICCO (1991), *'Prospects for the World Cocoa Market until the Year 2005'*, Report by the UNCTAD secretariat and the secretariat of the International Cocoa Organization (United Nations, New York)

Vogelvang, E. (1988), *'A Quarterly Econometric Model of the World Coffee Economy'*, Free University Press, Amsterdam.

Westlake, M. J. (1977), *ODI Review*, 2, Overseas Development Institute, London.

World Bank (1995), *Commodity Markets and the Developing Countries* (quarterly), Washington, DC.

Yeboah, D. (1992), 'Forecasting Coffee Consumption with a Flexible Consumer Demand Function', *UNCTAD Review*, 3: 71–96, UNCTAD, Geneva

Index

Note: Page numbers with n indicate footnotes